Taxcafe.co.uk Tax Guides

Tax Saving Tactics for Non-Doms

By Lee Hadnum LLB ACA CTA

Important Legal Notices:

Taxcafe®
Tax Guide - "Tax Saving Tactics for Non-Doms"

Published by:
Taxcafe UK Limited
67 Milton Road
Kirkcaldy KY1 1TL
Tel: (0044) 01592 560081
Email: team@taxcafe.co.uk

ISBN   978-1-907302-20-6

Fourth edition, July 2010

Trademarks
Taxcafe® is a registered trademark of Taxcafe UK Limited. All other logos, trademarks, names and logos in this tax guide may be trademarks of their respective owners.

Disclaimer
Before reading or relying on the content of this tax guide please read the disclaimer carefully. If you have any queries then please contact the publisher at team@taxcafe.co.uk.

Disclaimer

1. Please note that this Tax Guide is intended as **general guidance only** for individual readers and does NOT constitute accountancy, tax, investment or other professional advice. Neither Taxcafe UK Limited nor the author can accept any responsibility or liability for loss which may arise from reliance on information contained in this Tax Guide.

2. Please note that tax legislation, the law and practices by government and regulatory authorities (e.g. Revenue & Customs) are constantly changing. We therefore recommend that for accountancy, tax, investment or other professional advice, you consult a suitably qualified accountant, tax specialist, independent financial adviser, or other professional adviser. Please also note that your personal circumstances may vary from the general examples contained in this Tax Guide and your professional adviser will be able to give specific advice based on your personal circumstances.

3. This Tax Guide covers taxation applying to UK residents only. Please note that references to the 'UK' do not include the Channel Islands or the Isle of Man. The tax position of non-UK residents is beyond the scope of this Tax Guide.

4. Whilst in an effort to be helpful, this Tax Guide may refer to general guidance on matters other than the taxation of UK residents, neither Taxcafe UK Limited nor the author are expert in these matters. Neither Taxcafe UK Limited nor the author can accept any responsibility or liability for loss which may arise from reliance on such information contained in this Tax Guide.

5. Please note that Taxcafe UK Limited has relied wholly on the expertise of the author in the preparation of the content of this Tax Guide. The author is not an employee of Taxcafe UK Limited but has been selected by Taxcafe UK Limited using reasonable care and skill to write the content of this Tax Guide.

6. All persons described in the examples in this guide are entirely fictional characters created specifically for the purposes of this guide. Any similarities to actual persons, living or dead, or to fictional characters created by any other author, are entirely coincidental.

Other Taxcafe guides by the same author

Non-Resident & Offshore Tax Planning

The World's Best Tax Havens

Using a Company to Save Tax

The Investor's Tax Bible

Selling Your Business

About the Author

Lee Hadnum is a key member of the Taxcafe team. Apart from authoring a number of our tax guides, he also provides personalised tax advice through our popular Question & Answer Service, a role he carries out with a great deal of enthusiasm and professionalism.

Lee is a rarity among tax advisers having both legal AND chartered accountancy qualifications. After qualifying as a prize winner in the Institute of Chartered Accountants entrance exams, he went on to become a Chartered Tax Adviser (CTA).

Having worked in Ernst & Young's tax department for a number of years, Lee decided to start his own tax consulting firm, specialising in capital gains tax, inheritance tax and business tax planning. He now provides online guidance and unique tax planning reports at www.wealthprotectionreport.co.uk and www.tax-bids.com.

Lee has taken his own advice and now lives overseas himself. Whenever he has spare time he enjoys DIY, walking and travelling.

Contents

Chapter 1

Introduction

Big changes to the tax treatment of people who are not UK domiciled (also known as non-doms) were announced in the October 2007 Pre-Budget Report. Further tax changes have also been made in subsequent Budgets.

As a result of all the chopping and changing, many non-domiciled individuals are not entirely sure how the new rules will affect them in practice. However, we're confident we will answer most of your questions in this guide.

The main changes have applied since April 6th 2008. The current tax regime for non-doms is far more restrictive than the old one. However, there are still tax benefits to be had from being non UK domiciled.

Our purpose is to explain all the changes in plain English and, most important of all, show you how you can still use your non-domiciled status to reduce your UK tax bill.

Scope of this Guide

The aim of this guide is to give you a thorough grounding in non-domicile tax issues. Please note that it does not cover **every** eventuality – that would be impossible in a general guide of this nature. So please bear in mind the general nature of the information contained here.

Individual circumstances vary so it's always vital to get professional advice before you do anything that may have tax consequences.

After reading this guide, however, we are confident that you will have a firm grasp of how non-domiciled people are taxed and

1

what you can do to pay less tax on your overseas income and capital gains.

As for jargon, there isn't very much of it you'll be pleased to hear.

Most of the time we refer to non-domiciled individuals as 'non-doms'. We sometimes refer to capital gains tax as just CGT. You may also see us talk about the 'taxman' when referring to HM Revenue & Customs, also known as HMRC.

Tax is all about tax years and some of the examples have dates in them. The UK is one of the few remaining countries that has a tax year which doesn't run from January to December. Our tax year runs from 6th April in one year to 5th April the next year.

Chapter 2

What is Domicile?

So what does domicile mean exactly?

Your domicile is essentially the country you regard as your permanent home. If you don't live there at present, you must intend to return there one day.

Domicile status has been an important part of the UK tax system for well over 100 years, although it's not just a tax concept. Its main purpose is determining legal 'connection' and deciding whether UK or foreign law applies in various situations. Most notably your domicile status determines how your estate will be 'divvied up' when you die. Various UK laws contain specific exceptions for non-domiciled people.

The main tax benefit of being non-domiciled has always been that you are entitled to the so-called 'remittance basis'. This generally means UK tax is only paid on your overseas income and capital gains when the money is brought back into the UK.

Other UK residents always pay tax on the 'arising basis'. This means you pay tax on your worldwide income and gains each year. It doesn't matter whether you bring the money into the UK or leave it abroad.

The new rules have made the remittance basis less attractive for many non-doms but there are still tax savings to be had, as we'll see shortly.

You may be interested to know that the remittance basis used to be available to everyone living in the UK but the concession was removed gradually over a number of years. Since the mid 1970s only non-domiciled individuals and those not ordinarily resident in the UK have qualified for this tax concession.

The 2008 changes are therefore the latest in a very long line of amendments and clampdowns.

The 3 Types of Domicile

There are three main types of domicile:

- **Domicile of Origin**. This is acquired when you're born and is usually your father's domicile. If your parents are unmarried, it's your mother's domicile. Domicile of origin continues unless you acquire a new domicile of choice.

- **Domicile of Choice**. You acquire a domicile of choice by voluntarily making a new country your permanent home with the intention of remaining there for the rest of your days.

- **Domicile of Dependency**. This type of domicile only applies to children under the age of 16. It only comes into the picture if there's a change in the father's domicile (or mother if the parents were unmarried). If this happens, the parent's new domicile of choice becomes the child's domicile of dependency.

UK Immigrants and Emigrants

In practice, there are mainly two types of non-domiciled people:

- Firstly, there are foreign nationals who come to live in the UK. They usually have a foreign domicile of origin, and provided they don't acquire a UK domicile of choice, will usually remain non-domiciled. Their children will generally also be non-domiciled, even if they were born in the UK and are UK nationals, provided they don't establish the UK as their domicile of choice.

4

- Secondly, there are UK nationals who have a UK domicile of origin and decide to emigrate. If they leave the UK permanently they may wish to establish a new domicile of choice overseas. If they succeed they'll become non UK domiciled.

If you leave the UK permanently you will also lose your UK resident status and will generally not have to pay UK income tax and capital gains tax. The extra benefit of losing your UK domicile is that you will also be exempt from UK inheritance tax on your overseas assets.

It's the first group – foreign nationals and their offspring living in the UK – that we'll focus on in this guide and it's this group that the new tax laws are aimed at.

Recent Case Law on Domicile

If you are to lose your overseas domicile of origin and instead be classed as having made the UK your domicile of choice, there are two key conditions to be satisfied:

- Firstly, there is a requirement to have residence in the UK and
- Secondly, you need to have an intention to live in the UK permanently or indefinitely

This was considered in a case before the Court of Appeal in 2008 (*Henwood v Barlow Clowes International Ltd*). In this case the judge said:

"...What has to be proved is no mere inclination arising from a passing fancy or thrust upon a man by an external but temporary pressure, but an intention freely formed to reside in a certain territory indefinitely. All the elements of the intention must be shown to exist if the change is to be established: if any one element is not proved, the case for a change fails..."

This therefore reinforces just how serious a change in domicile is.

The judge also said:

"...It seems to me that as a general proposition the acquisition of any new domicile should in general always be treated as a serious allegation because of its serious consequences..."

Residence

One of the requirements is that you establish a residence in the UK.

Essentially this means that you need to establish a home in the UK. Residence in this context doesn't necessarily mean tax residence but has a wider scope to include your main residence.

If you have more than one home in different countries the position is less clear and you need to look for the sole or chief residence.

This was reinforced in this case where the judge said:

"...Since a person can only have one domicile, it is necessary to identify which of the countries in which he has a home, if he has more than one, is the country of his domicile."

Determining which is the chief or principal residence involves considering the quality of your residence in the various countries.

For instance in *IRC v Duchess of Portland* where the individual had residences in Canada and England, where she lived with her husband, the judge held that the court had to consider in which country she was an inhabitant.

In *Plummer v IRC* the individual in question had a domicile of origin in England but her family had moved to Guernsey.

She remained in England principally for the purpose of completing her education.

She intended, when she had finished her training and had some experience working in this country, to return to Guernsey, where she spent part of her time.

The judge held that the Special Commissioners were entitled to say that her chief residence was in England and that, as she had her chief residence in England, which was her domicile of origin, she had not acquired a domicile of choice in Guernsey.

Intention

This is where the taxpayer got caught out in the Henwood case.

Although this case was concerned with a UK domiciliary losing UK domicile by moving overseas (ie the exact opposite to where someone has a foreign domicile who is looking to move to the UK and not establish a UK domicile of choice), it is still useful to understand how the courts approach the issue of domicile.

In this case the judge held that where a person maintained homes in more than one country, his domicile had to be decided by reference to the quality of residence in each of those countries to ascertain in which country he had an intention permanently to reside.

Therefore you would need to ensure that if you did have multiple homes that you retained an intention to return overseas.

In the Henwood case they looked at the individual's actual lifestyle in the various countries (Mauritius and France in this case) to assess the quality of his residence:

"...So the question is whether Mr Henwood has established on a balance of probabilities that he has a domicile of choice in Mauritius. He has

had a residence there for many years. But it is the quality of his residence that matters and thus he has in effect to show that he preferred Mauritius to any other place in the world. He said that was so, but then of course these were self-serving statements.

He clearly had a very comfortable and convenient residence in France. He chose to say that France was not his domicile of choice, but in my judgment, he still had to provide a satisfactory answer to this further question: if France was not his domicile of choice, what did Mauritius have for him that France did not and that clearly enabled the court to say that he had chosen to settle in Mauritius in preference to any other place where he customarily resided?

For my part, I would not accept as a reason that he liked island life. He also liked French wine and culture. I have considered the relevant factors above and none of them in my judgment provides an answer to the question I have posed. In reality, if he did not consider that France was his domicile of choice, it is unlikely that Mauritius was…"

This case reinforces just how close your ties have to be to a country to support a change in domicile. It also makes clear just how difficult it can be to show a change from a domicile of origin to a domicile of choice (which is arguably good news for foreign domiciliaries moving to the UK!)

Simply having a strong presence in the country in itself will not be enough. Your residence and intention are also important factors.

Protecting Your Foreign Domicile

If you're a foreign national living in the UK, retaining your non-domiciled status is of key importance.

As we've seen above this means making sure you keep your domicile of origin and do not acquire a UK domicile of choice.

It's not as difficult as it sounds, and most foreign nationals will retain their foreign domicile.

If Revenue & Customs wanted to argue otherwise, the burden of proof would be on them and they would need to show that you had made the UK your sole or 'chief' residence and intend to remain here for the rest of your days.

It's difficult for the taxman to do this if a non-dom actually asserts the opposite! In practice, keeping overseas ties is the best evidence of a desire to return to your home country one day. This would include:

- Joining clubs and other social organisations in your home country.
- Holding assets in your home country
- Having bank accounts overseas
- Buying an overseas burial plot
- Subscribing to overseas newspapers
- Purchasing property abroad
- Making a will under the laws of your home country
- Retaining friends and family connections in your home country
- Visiting the home country occasionally

As stated earlier, a non-dom's children will also typically 'inherit' their father's overseas domicile of origin. Therefore they can also establish non UK domiciled status, even if they're UK born and bred.

It's vital though that they do not become UK domiciled by having the UK classed as their new permanent home. This is a risk many face. If they have few overseas ties (they may have never even visited the home country), they run the risk of being classed as UK domiciled in the future.

For most, however, this risk is probably more apparent than real. The non UK domicile will be kept, provided the ultimate intention is to return overseas. Anything they can do to support this intention would be invaluable, in the event that the taxman argues they are UK domiciled. This could include visiting to the home country, reading local newspapers, opening an overseas bank account etc.

Chapter 3

Summary of Non-Dom Tax Benefits

In this section we're going to briefly summarize the tax benefits of being non UK domiciled. After that we'll take a closer look at the new rules which apply from April 6th 2008.

Inheritance Tax

Non-domiciled people only pay inheritance tax on their UK assets. Overseas assets escape UK inheritance tax. There's no change to this rule from April 6th 2008.

Capital Gains Tax and Income Tax

If you're UK resident and UK domiciled you have to pay income tax and capital gains tax on your worldwide income and capital gains. So if you sell overseas property or earn interest from an overseas bank account it will be subject to UK tax, whether you leave the money overseas or bring it into the UK.

This is known as the arising basis. Your income is taxed when it arises. You do not have to actually receive it in the UK to be taxed on it.

If you're UK resident but not UK domiciled you enjoy more choice. You can be taxed under either the arising basis or the remittance basis. With the remittance basis the basic idea is you only pay tax when you actually bring the money into the UK.

Of course, you may have to pay foreign tax, so it's not always possible for non-doms to have tax-free overseas investments. Foreign tax can usually be deducted from your UK tax bill.

It should also be pointed out that it's not just non-doms who can benefit from the remittance basis. Individuals who are non-UK ordinarily resident can also claim the remittance basis, so the new rules will affect them as well.

So what does it mean to be non-UK ordinarily resident?

Mostly these are people who come to the UK to work for a while. They're usually treated as not ordinarily resident if it's clear they intend to stay in the UK for less than three years. This means they usually enjoy a three year window during which they can claim the remittance basis.

This is not, however ,always the case and HMRC can argue that an individual is UK ordinarily resident where they are in the UK for a fixed and settled purpose. We've looked at this in detail, including the impact of a recent 2010 case in our offshore tax planning guide *"Non Resident & Offshore Tax Planning"*.

The UK remittance rules have become more complicated since April 6th 2008 but what we can say is that if you're a non-dom or non-UK ordinarily resident, you have more flexibility than other people and this allows you to do some useful tax planning.

The changes are going to mainly affect non-doms living in the UK. People who emigrate from the UK will be outside the scope of most UK income and capital gains taxes regardless of their domicile status because they are non resident.

Deemed Domicile

Before we move on it's essential to make one important point about non-doms and inheritance tax.

As we know, non-doms still have to pay inheritance tax on their UK assets but they don't have to pay inheritance tax on their overseas assets.

However, this tax concession doesn't last forever. There are some 'deemed domicile' rules that apply purely for inheritance tax purposes.

Under these rules you're deemed to have a UK domicile:

- If you've lost your UK domicile within the last three years, or
- You've been UK resident for 17 out of the last 20 years.

The first rule is for people who emigrate and abandon their UK domicile. These people will still be subject to inheritance tax on their worldwide assets for the first three years but after that they don't have to pay inheritance tax on their overseas assets.

This group is not the focus of this guide, however. We're focusing on people who live in the UK and are non-UK domiciled. The second rule is more important for them. What it says is that if you're non-domiciled but you've been resident in the UK for at least 17 of the last 20 years, your overseas assets will now fall into the inheritance tax net.

Crucially though this won't have any impact on your domicile status for income tax or capital gains tax purposes.

For income tax and capital gains tax purposes no matter how long you've lived in the UK you can still retain non-dom status, provided you don't actually change your intention and decide to live in the UK permanently.

Non-doms have enjoyed huge UK tax savings in recent years by holding their investments overseas. The popular press made a big play of this, saying there was one set of tax rules for the rich and another for everybody else. This, together with proposals put forward by opposition parties, finally spurred the Government into action towards the end of 2007.

Let's take a look at these changes.

Chapter 4

The Main Tax Changes

There have been big changes to the way the remittance basis has operated since April 6th 2008.

It's important to stress that the new rules will not affect your non-domiciled status. However, they will affect how you can benefit from using this status.

Income and Gains Earned Before April 6th 2008

It's also important to stress that the new rules only apply to income and gains earned from April 6th 2008.

All the money you earned before that date can be kept overseas tax free and will only be taxed if you bring it into the UK.

For example, if you earned £5,000 of interest on your overseas bank account in 2007, you can keep that money overseas tax free. You will only pay tax when you transfer it into your UK bank account.

The key changes that apply from April 6th 2008 are as follows:

Choice Between Remittance or Arising Basis

From now on you must make a choice every year between the remittance basis and the arising basis.

Under the remittance basis you qualify for special tax treatment if you decide to keep your income and gains overseas. The arising basis is the way most UK residents are taxed and means you pay tax immediately, regardless of whether you keep the money overseas or bring it into the UK.

In the past non-doms were automatically taxed on the remittance basis in some cases. Now you'll have to actively claim to be taxed this way. If you don't, you'll automatically be taxed on the arising basis. This was also confirmed in the 2009 Budget, when the Chancellor announced that the legislation would be amended to make this fact extra clear.

Because they can make a different choice every year, non-doms have flexibility to do some constructive tax planning.

Special Concession

The new rules contain one very important concession for the first chunk of overseas income you earn. If your unremitted income and gains are less than £2,000, the remittance basis applies automatically.

If you keep within this limit you effectively 'fall under the radar' and your overseas income and gains can be kept offshore and tax free. Note that for your tax return you will, however, need to tick boxes 27 and 28 of the remittance pages to take advantage of this special rule (see Chapter 5).

If you are a higher-rate taxpayer, this concession could save you £799.60 in tax every year:

$$£1,999 \times 40\% \text{ tax} = £799.60$$

And if you are married and your spouse is also non-domiciled the total potential tax saving is £1,599:

$$£1,999 \times 2 \times 40\% = £1,599$$

You'll notice we use the number £1,999. That's because your unremitted overseas income must be under £2,000. If you have

£2,000 or more of unremitted income, you do not qualify at all for this concession.

The concession is more generous than it appears. A non-dom who earns, say, 3% interest in an overseas bank account can effectively keep almost £67,000 offshore and out of the UK taxman's clutches. A married couple who are both non-domiciled can keep almost £134,000 offshore and not worry about UK tax.

You can get your hands on these tax savings by simply spending the money when you travel abroad.

Everyone Qualifies for the Exemption

It's important to point out that you can benefit from this concession even if your total overseas income exceeds £1,999.

What matters is how much "unremitted overseas income" you have, not your total overseas income.

So as long as you remit the rest of your income and gains to the UK and pay tax you will still qualify.

For example, if you earn £10,000 overseas interest during the year, you can remit £8,001 to the UK and pay tax on it and keep £1,999 offshore and tax free.

It's also important to point out that all non-doms qualify for this concession, no matter how long they've lived in the UK.

Other non-dom tax concessions are taken away after you've been living in the UK for a certain length of time.

The 2009 Budget further extended the provisions to ensure that the remittance basis applies automatically where a non-dom has total UK income or gains of no more than £100 which have been taxed in the UK, provided they make no remittances to the UK during the tax year.

Small Amounts of Foreign Employment Income

There is a separate exemption for any non-doms who have overseas employment income.

Individuals employed in the UK are usually required to file a tax return if they have also received income from overseas employment in the same tax year. However, in practice if the employment income is subject to foreign tax there's unlikely to be any significant UK tax liability as the foreign tax will reduce the UK liability.

Therefore HMRC provide an exemption so that non-doms won't need to file a return as long as they meet the following conditions:

1. They have income from a UK-based employment
2. If they have foreign earnings, these amount to £10,000 or less and are subject to a foreign tax.
3. If they have any foreign bank interest the amount of interest is £100 or less. Again this interest must be subject to a foreign tax.
4. They have no other foreign income and gains for the tax year.
5. They are subject to UK income tax only at the basic rate (or starting rate for savings income).

If all of these conditions apply, the individual receives an effective exemption from UK income tax on the foreign income and would not need to complete a tax return.

Cases of Overlap

It's important to note that this exemption for anyone with small amounts of foreign employment income applies the arising basis for the year, but provides an exemption for the foreign income so that no tax return is required.

This is completely different to the exemption which applies the remittance basis automatically to unremitted foreign income of less than £2,000.

There could easily be cases of overlap with this exemption for employment income and the exemption for unremitted foreign income of less than £2,000 (eg where you had only £1,500 foreign unremitted employment income, all subject to foreign tax).

In this case the exemption for the foreign employment income takes priority and the arising basis applies. If you did want to use the remittance basis you would need to file a tax return and claim it.

Establishing Non UK Domiciled Status

Even though you may be pretty sure that you are non UK domiciled, actually establishing this can be a different matter.

For many, inheritance tax (IHT) will be a big issue. If you're non-domiciled your overseas estate can be excluded from UK IHT, whereas a UK domiciliary is not so lucky and will pay tax on overseas assets as well.

The last thing you may want is the taxman questioning your domicile status after you've gone, leaving your beneficiaries to sort it all out.

One way to establish your domicile status with Revenue & Customs during your lifetime would be to have overseas unremitted income (for example, bank interest) that is less than £2,000.

There's then no loss of allowances or need to pay the £30,000 tax charge. You'll still, however, be declaring your position as a non UK domiciliary.

As a non UK domiciliary with unremitted overseas income of less than £2,000 you're entitled to the remittance basis automatically.

Note that if you were a UK domiciliary this income would be taxed in the UK. This means that your domicile status is directly relevant in determining your tax liability. As such the taxman will either accept (or not accept!) your domicile status.

Claiming the Remittance Basis – What You Lose

If you want to be taxed on the remittance basis you have to say so on your tax return. Otherwise you'll be taxed on the arising basis.

So why won't all non-doms choose to be taxed on the remittance basis? Well the Government has introduced two hefty tax penalties to reduce its attractiveness.

The first penalty is you lose various tax allowances and exemptions. These include the:

- Income tax personal allowance
- Blind person's allowance
- Married couples reductions
- Capital gains tax annual exemption
- Tax relief for life insurance payments

It's important to note that you also lose these allowances for your UK income and gains, not just your overseas income and gains.

This penalty applies to ALL non-doms who claim the remittance basis, no matter how long they have lived in the UK.

For most people the biggest punishments will be the loss of the income tax personal allowance and annual capital gains tax exemption. Your personal allowance currently shelters the first £6,475 of your income from tax and the capital gains tax exemption shelters the first £10,100 of your capital gains from tax.

So if you claim the remittance basis you may save tax on your overseas income but you could pay an extra £2,590 in UK income tax if you are a higher-rate taxpayer. That's because:

$$£6,475 \times 40\% \text{ tax} = £2,590$$

And if you have also sold shares, property or other assets you could pay an extra £2,828 in capital gains tax if you lose your annual CGT exemption. That's because:

$$£10,100 \times 28\% = £2,828$$

Note that the rate of capital gains tax you will pay depends on when you sold the asset. Disposals between 6 April 2008 and 22 June 2010 are taxed at a flat rate of 18%. Disposals after 22 June 2010 are taxed at 18% if you are a basic-rate taxpayer and 28% if you are a higher-rate taxpayer.

The loss of the married couples allowance will make little difference to most people. It would only apply if you or your spouse was born before 6th April 1935 and would then provide a tax saving of just a few hundred pounds.

Another relief that is lost by claiming the remittance basis is the relief for life insurance payments. This will not affect all non-doms. Where this relief applies it allows tax relief to be claimed for payments deducted from your salary for providing benefits for your children (and your spouse in certain cases) if you die.

However, the maximum tax relief is fixed at just £100, so the loss of this relief won't be a major concern for most people.

The £30,000 Sting

The second drawback of claiming the remittance basis – and this is the one that has been given the most publicity – is the annual £30,000 tax charge.

This only comes into play if:

- You claim the remittance basis on your tax return, and

- You've been UK resident for at least 7 of the previous 9 tax years.

This £30,000 tax charge is what most non-doms fear the most. You can avoid it by simply opting for the arising basis and paying UK income tax and capital gains tax on your overseas income and capital gains.

It also won't apply if you don't actually have to claim the remittance basis because your unremitted income and capital gains are less than £2,000.

If you do opt for the remittance basis, the £30,000 charge applies only if you've been UK resident for 7 or more of the last 9 years.

This gives foreign nationals who have newly arrived in the UK a 7 year 'honeymoon' period in which they can use the remittance basis without having to pay the £30,000 tax charge.

They will still, however, lose their various income tax allowances and CGT exemption if they choose the remittance basis.

The Honeymoon Period

The £30,000 tax charge only applies to non-doms who have been UK resident for at least 7 of the previous 9 years.

Note the honeymoon is based on tax years and any part years will count as one whole year.

Remember tax years run from April to April. The tax year running from 6th April 2010 to 5th April 2011 would typically be written as 2010/11.

Example

Let's say Denise came to the UK in June 2003 and was classed as UK resident from that date.

She would therefore be classed as UK resident for the following tax years:

1. 2003/04 (remember part years count as full years of residence)
2. 2004/05
3. 2005/06
4. 2006/07
5. 2007/08
6. 2008/09
7. 2009/10

Denise wants to know if she has to pay the £30,000 charge during the current 2010/11 tax year. She will have to pay the charge if she has been UK resident for at least 7 of the previous 9 tax years. We can see that she has been UK resident for the previous 7 years and therefore has to pay the charge if she claims the remittance basis for the 2010/11 tax year.

Another way of looking at it is to say that you are subject to the £30,000 charge if *including the current tax year* you have been resident for 8 or more out of the last 10 tax years.

The reason we mention this is because sometimes you will hear people referring to 7 years of residence and sometimes to 8. It just depends on whether you are including the current tax year as well.

In this example, including the current 2010/11 tax year, Denise has been resident for the last 8 tax years and therefore has to pay the £30,000 charge.

Remember also that the years of residence do not have to be consecutive.

Example

Let's say Pedro is non-domiciled and was UK resident in some tax years but non-resident in others, as follows:

2001/02	Resident
2002/03	Resident
2003/04	Non Resident
2004/05	Non Resident
2005/06	Resident
2006/07	Resident
2007/08	Resident
2008/09	Resident
2009/10	Resident
2010/11	Resident

For the 2010/11 tax year Pedro will look back at the last 10 years to 2001/2002 and count up how many years he has been UK resident. In this case, including 2010/2011, he has been resident for 8 years and therefore has to pay the £30,000 charge if he claims the remittance basis for the current tax year.

Summary

- If your unremitted overseas income or gains for the year are **under** £2,000 you can keep them offshore and not pay any UK tax.

- If your unremitted income and gains are £2,000 or more you can keep them offshore and not pay any tax but you will lose your income tax personal allowance, your CGT exemption and various other allowances.

- If your income and gains are £2,000 or more and you have been living in the UK for at least 7 of the previous 9 tax years you can keep them offshore but you will lose your income tax personal allowance, your CGT exemption and will have to pay the £30,000 charge.

Chapter 5

Completing Your Tax Return

Completing your tax return can be complicated if you are non domiciled. There are essentially four separate forms that you may need to complete:

Firstly, there is the main tax return itself:

www.hmrc.gov.uk/forms/sa100.pdf

Secondly, there are the residence and remittance basis supplementary pages:

www.hmrc.gov.uk/forms/sa109.pdf

Thirdly, there are the foreign supplementary pages:

www.hmrc.gov.uk/forms/sa106.pdf

Finally, there are the capital gains supplementary pages:

www.hmrc.gov.uk/forms/sa108.pdf

We have based this chapter on the tax return for the tax year running from 6 April 2009 to 5 April 2010 – the most recent one available at the date of publication.

The Main Tax Return

Completing the relevant non-dom boxes on the main tax return is actually pretty straightforward. The special supplementary pages usually only have to be completed if you are using the remittance basis.

You would need to tick 'Yes' to box 8 on page TR2 (illustrated below) if you used the remittance basis during the tax year in question.

So even if you had overseas unremitted income or gains of less than £2,000 you would still need to tick 'Yes'.

If you did not use the remittance basis then you would tick 'No' and usually would not need to provide any specific disclosures with respect to your non-dom status. This would not prevent you from claiming the remittance basis in future years.

> **8** Residence, remittance basis etc.
> Were you, for all or part of the year to 5 April 2010, one or more of the following - not resident, not ordinarily resident or not domiciled in the UK and claiming the remittance basis; or dual resident in the UK and another country?
>
> Yes ☐   No ☐

The Residence and Remittance Pages

You only have to complete this form if you are using the remittance basis.

The *Domicile* section starts off by asking if being domiciled outside the UK is relevant to your income tax or capital gains tax liability (see below)

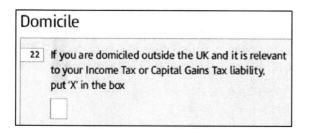

> # Domicile
>
> **22** If you are domiciled outside the UK and it is relevant to your Income Tax or Capital Gains Tax liability, put 'X' in the box
>
> ☐

This would usually only be the case if you were UK resident but non UK domiciled and you had overseas unremitted income or gains and wished to use the remittance basis.

This box would therefore need to be ticked even if you had under £2,000 of overseas unremitted income or gains.

If, however, you were non domiciled but had no overseas unremitted income or gains or just wanted to claim the arising basis you would not tick box 22, and would then leave the other boxes blank as well.

You would then be taxed on the arising basis and would enter all your UK and overseas income and gains on your tax return.

If you were using the remittance basis you would tick box 22 and also complete boxes 23-26 as appropriate (these ask for details regarding the date you became non UK domiciled).

You would then need to actually claim the remittance basis on your tax return by putting an 'X' in box 27 (see below).

Box 27 would be ticked in all cases where you want to use the remittance basis. You would then lose your annual CGT exemption and personal allowance, unless you had overseas unremitted income or gains of less than £2,000.

In that case you would also need to tick box 28 to ensure that you do not lose these allowances.

Box 29 will be ticked if you have been UK resident for 7 or more of the 9 previous tax years. In that case you would then be liable for the £30,000 remittance tax charge, unless you were under 18. You would need to tick box 30 if you were aged under 18.

27	If you are making a claim for the remittance basis for 2009-10, put 'X' in the box
	☐

28	If your unremitted income and capital gains for 2009-10 is less than £2,000, put 'X' in the box
	☐

29	If you were UK resident for 2009-10 and for seven or more of the preceding nine tax years, put 'X' in the box
	☐

30	If you were under 18 on 5 April 2010, put 'X' in the box
	☐

If you are liable to pay the £30,000 remittance tax charge there are also a number of additional boxes that you will need to complete:

31	Amount of nominated income
	£ ⬚⬚⬚⬚⬚⬚⬚⬚⬚ · 0 0

32	Amount of nominated capital gains
	£ ⬚⬚⬚⬚⬚⬚⬚⬚⬚ · 0 0

33	Adjustment to payments on account
	£ ⬚⬚⬚⬚⬚⬚⬚⬚⬚ · ⬚⬚

34	If you have remitted any nominated income or gains during 2009-10, put 'X' in the box
	☐

These boxes require details of the amount of overseas income and capital gains that you have nominated to apply against the £30,000 tax charge. It's essential that you track these separately and provide details of any future remittances of nominated income or gains. If you have remitted nominated income or gains from previous years you would need to tick box 34 and enter details in the blank space in box 35.

By claiming the remittance basis you would then only enter details of overseas income or capital gains actually remitted into the UK on your UK tax return. As such, if you retained all your overseas income or gains abroad you would not provide details of these income/gains on your tax return.

If you did remit overseas income or gains you need to complete:

- The foreign pages in respect of any income that was remitted to the UK: www.hmrc.gov.uk/forms/sa106.pdf

- The capital gains pages for any overseas capital gains remitted to the UK: www.hmrc.gov.uk/forms/sa108.pdf

You enter remittances from both the current year and any previous years in these pages as well.

Special Concession: Non-Doms with No UK Income

The legislation does contain a special provision which protects certain individuals who use the remittance basis from having to complete a tax return. Anyone who is entitled to claim the remittance basis and who:

- Has no UK income or gains, and
- Doesn't remit any foreign income or gains,

does not have to submit a tax return to claim the remittance basis, provided they're not subject to the £30,000 tax charge.

This applies even if there is unremitted overseas income of more than £2,000.

Example

Maria came to the UK with her husband Mario in 2006. Her husband works in the City. Maria is a housewife and has no UK income or capital gains. However she does have overseas dividends of £15,000 per year which she keeps overseas.

She will not need to complete a UK tax return because, although she has more than £2,000 of unremitted income, she:

- Has no UK income or capital gains
- Does not remit any of the income to the UK
- Is not subject to the £30,000 annual tax charge

Therefore there is no UK tax to pay and she does not have to complete a tax return.

Once she has been in the UK for 8 tax years, however, she will have to complete a return.

Overseas Employment Income

As stated previously there is also an exemption for overseas employment income.

If you have:

- Overseas employment income of less than £10,000, and
- Overseas bank interest of less than £100,

you will not have to file a UK tax return, provided the overseas income is subject to foreign tax.

What You Have to Disclose to the Taxman

When the original draft legislation was released there was widespread concern that non-doms would be forced to disclose income and capital gains for a number of previous years.

This was not popular as many non-doms prize confidentiality just as highly as tax savings. The prospect of having their overseas income and assets disclosed to overseas tax authorities in accordance with the UK's double tax treaty network was a serious bone of contention.

The Revenue issued a statement in 2008 to clarify the treatment which stated:

"...those using the remittance basis will not be required to make any additional disclosures about their income and gains arising abroad. So long as they declare their remittances to the UK and pay UK tax on them, they will not be required to disclose information on the source of the remittances..."

This is in line with the existing position and effectively states that provided all remittances are declared, there is no further requirement to disclose the source of the funds remitted or the overseas income. The non-dom tax return pages confirm this – there is no requirement to disclose the source of unremitted income and gains.

Therefore if the remittance basis is chosen you will not usually need to declare the source of the overseas income or gains that are not remitted.

However, you still have to keep track of the overseas income or gains. In particular, if you have overseas mixed funds or nominated income accounts HMRC may look for details of overseas income or gains when assessing the tax position of remittances from these accounts.

In addition, if you make the foreign capital loss election (we look at this shortly) this could open up extra opportunities for HMRC to ask for details of overseas capital gains.

Limits for Tax Returns & Enquiries

There are a couple of limits that HMRC applies in practice to non-doms. Note that you won't find any of these limits in the tax legislation.

These are applied by HMRC purely as a matter of practice. However, these practices have been published and as such can usually be relied upon by taxpayers.

Unremitted Income and Gains Less than £2,000

We've stated earlier in the guide that where a non-dom has total unremitted foreign income and gains of less than £2,000 in any tax year, they can use the remittance basis without having to make a formal claim by submitting a tax return. The advantage of this is no loss of the UK personal allowance or their annual capital gains tax exemption and no requirement to pay the £30,000 remittance charge.

Note that this exemption applies to unremitted income or gains of less than £2,000. So you could have overseas income of £10,000, and remit £8,500. Your unremitted income would then be less than £2,000 and you would not need to pay the £30,000 tax charge and could still offset your UK personal allowance. However, in this case you're still taxable on any foreign income or gains remitted to the UK. Remittances can be in the form of cash, assets or services enjoyed in the UK.

So in the example above the £8,500 remittance would be taxed in the UK and would need to be included on a self assessment tax return.

If you weren't currently within the self-assessment regime you would need to file a return reporting the remittances (and paying tax on them).

But what if you were only remitting a small amount and have no other taxable income?

HMRC has made provision for small cash remittances to the UK to be free of tax and also free of reporting requirements.

The idea is to help people on low incomes and to ensure that they don't need to complete a tax return just to show the remittances where only a small amount of tax is due.

HMRC has said that, where the £2,000 exemption applies, if an individual remits cash of less than £500 in total into the UK during the tax year, which arises from foreign income or gains, there is no requirement to submit a self-assessment tax return simply to pay the tax on those cash remittances.

This means that an individual could have unremitted income of £2,498 and remit £499 without there being a tax charge and no requirement to file a UK tax return and no loss of the UK allowances or a requirement to pay the £30,000 remittance charge.

This can be doubled for a couple.

Note, however, that the ability not to disclose on a return only applies if the individual would not otherwise need to file a return. If they would need to file a tax return anyway they would need to include the remittances on the return and pay the tax due.

Establishing Non-Dom Status – Trust Transfers

For any non-doms leaving the UK and looking to establish non UK domicile status, the options for getting HMRC's agreement during your lifetime are limited.

A common way to get HMRC to consider your domicile status is to wait three tax years after leaving the UK and then make a transfer of overseas assets into an offshore trust. If you are non-domiciled there would be no inheritance tax (as the transfer would be of excluded property).

Individuals who transfer cash into offshore trusts and who consider themselves to be non UK domiciled are not required to submit an Inheritance Tax Account to HMRC (because if the settlor is non-UK domiciled, no inheritance tax is due).

However, if they do file an Inheritance Tax Account (IHT 100) HMRC may then consider the settlor's domicile status. Once established it will apply for income tax and capital gains tax purposes as well. Note, however, that any significant lifestyle changes by the individual could impact on his domicile status and could result in HMRC reconsidering the individual's domicile status.

When considering whether to look at an individual's domicile status HMRC will continue its existing practice and only open an enquiry into the return if the amounts of inheritance tax at stake make such an enquiry cost effective to carry out. At present that limit is £10,000.

So for the current year if you had the full nil rate band available you would need to be transferring just above £375,000. After the £325,000 nil rate band you would have £50,000 chargeable to IHT, with the IHT charge at 20% on lifetime transfers coming in at £10,000.

Chapter 6

How the £30,000 Charge Works in Practice

The £30,000 charge was announced in the October 2007 Pre-Budget Report but significant changes were made to how it operates in the March 2008 Budget and were finalised in the 2008 Finance Act.

Crucially it is not a separate stand-alone tax any more but is treated as a prepayment of income tax or capital gains tax.

By making it a regular income tax or capital gains tax charge this means it could qualify for double tax relief under many of the UK's double tax treaties.

For example, Revenue and Customs has published guidance on the treatment for US tax purposes which establishes that the £30,000 charge should be allowed as a credit against Federal income tax.

If you claim the remittance basis and are subject to the £30,000 charge, you have to nominate what income or capital gains it applies to. In the future that money can be remitted to the UK tax free.

Example

Jack is non-domiciled and has £20,000 tax to pay on his UK income. If he's claiming the remittance basis he'll need to nominate enough overseas income or capital gains to produce a total UK tax bill of £50,000:

£20,000 tax on UK income + £30,000 charge = £50,000

So the amount nominated must be enough to produce an additional £30,000 tax charge.

If the overseas income has already been taxed in another country, foreign tax paid would normally be allowed as a credit against your UK tax, so you would have to build that into the calculation as well.

Although income or gains that have been subjected to the £30,000 charge can then be remitted tax free, it's important to point out that there are also tough anti-avoidance rules if you also have money overseas that hasn't been taxed yet.

Any money you remit to the UK will be treated as being 'untaxed' money first. Only when you've brought in all your untaxed money and paid tax on it can you claim that you are bringing in money that has already been subject to the £30,000 charge.

Meticulous record keeping is the key because when you actually bring money into the UK, you will have to work out whether it has already been taxed or not.

Example

Let's take a look at an example of how the £30,000 charge works in practice. Edward has £100,000 of overseas income and decides to claim the remittance basis. He's a higher-rate taxpayer so would normally pay 40% or £40,000 in UK tax. So he opts for the remittance basis and pays the £30,000 charge.

He then needs to elect the overseas income to which the £30,000 tax applies. If he's a higher rate taxpayer this means that he could elect for overseas income of £75,000 to be treated as 'taxed' income. That's because:

$$£75,000 \times 40\% = £30,000$$

This means £75,000 of his overseas income can later be remitted to the UK tax free. This example assumes that no overseas tax has been paid.

However, £25,000 of his income still hasn't been taxed yet so the first £25,000 of any money he remits to the UK will be taxed – only after that will money sent to the UK be tax free.

When calculating your untaxed and taxed income you need to take account of the position for all tax years after April 2008.

So if Edward earned the same income of £100,000 for three tax years and nominated £75,000 per year as the taxed income, he would need to remit all of his untaxed income (3 x £25,000) before he could start bringing in the tax-free income.

Finally, it's important to point out that there is also an exemption from the £30,000 tax charge for minors.

Anyone under the age of 18 will not be subject to the £30,000 tax charge. There could therefore be some scope to transfer assets to non-domiciled children. We'll take a look at this shortly.

Nominating Income and Capital Gains

If you are claiming the remittance basis and are subject to the £30,000 tax charge you are required to make a nomination of your overseas income or gains for the tax year that will give rise to the £30,000 tax charge.

Strictly speaking the income (or gains) that are 'nominated' are subject to UK tax in that year on the arising basis, and are then regarded as 'taxed' income or gains. Therefore the nominated income/gains won't be taxed again if they are remitted in the future.

Therefore in the simple scenario you would nominate your overseas income to give rise to the £30,000 tax charge (say, £75,000).

You could then remit all of your other unremitted income and gains from (which would be taxed) and then when you finally remit your nominated £75,000 this would be free of UK tax.

However, the tax legislation includes provisions which penalise you if you try to remit the nominated amounts before you have remitted all other income and gains.

It does this by introducing strict ordering rules that lay down the nature of any remittance made if any nominated income or gains are brought into the UK while any foreign income or gains that were not nominated (after 6 April 2008) remain unremitted.

Essentially these rules ignore the nature of what was in fact remitted (capital gains or income) and instead treat the remittance as having been made in the least tax-efficient manner possible.

So even though you may actually be remitting unremitted capital gains (which could be taxed at 28% if you are a higher-rate taxpayer), if you have nominated income and other unremitted income you will be classed as remitting the unremitted income (potentially taxed at up to 50%).

Here's an example to show this key point:

Example

Steve is a non-dom and subject to the £30,000 tax charge. He has three offshore accounts that contain his foreign income and gains for the tax year.

In Year 1:

- Account A contains £75,000 of Steve's foreign investment income, just from that year.

- Account B contains £35,000 of Steve's foreign employment income from that year.

- Account C has some proceeds from an asset sale in that year, which includes £300,000 foreign chargeable gains.

Steve claims the remittance basis in Year 1 and nominates £75,000 of his foreign income in Account A. This is his nominated income.

After Year 1, Steve has no more foreign income/gains and leaves the accounts untouched.

In year 4 he brings £50,000 of his foreign income from Account A into the UK. This is a remittance of 'nominated income'. However, because he has other foreign income and gains from Year 1 that have not yet been remitted, the statutory ordering rules apply.

These will treat Steve as having remitted £35,000 of his foreign earnings from account B and then £15,000 of his foreign capital gains from Account C, even though he has not actually remitted any of this money.

In addition, because the rules look at all of an individual's foreign income or gains for a year, no consideration is given to any 'alienation' of those income or gains offshore at a later date. This includes occasions where the income or gains are used to pay for any foreign expenditure, such as personal spending while overseas.

So even if Steve has used his proceeds in Account C overseas, remittances of the final £25,000 from Account A would still be classed as a remittance of £25,000 of capital gain from Account C.

What this Means in Practice

Provided none of the nominated funds are ever remitted to the UK, you can continue to take advantage of the remittance basis in the usual manner in relation to your remaining funds.

Similarly if you're looking to remit all foreign unremitted income or gains and then the nominated income you can generally remit the nominated amounts free of UK tax.

However, if you're looking at remitting from the nominated account whilst you still have <u>any</u> unremitted foreign income or gains (based on the above very strict definition) this can have serious tax implications.

There are generally two key methods of funding the nominated account:

Full Nomination

The obvious option is to simply nominate sufficient overseas income or gains from the tax year in question that would give rise to a £30,000 UK tax charge.

So a higher-rate taxpayer for instance would nominate unremitted income of £75,000, capital gains of around £107,000 or a mixture of the two.

However, as we've seen above, by making a nomination of overseas income or gains this brings the statutory ordering rules into place and you would need to avoid any remittances from this nominated account where there is any other untaxed overseas income or gains.

Your remittances will be taxed as income first and only after that as capital gains. This could lead to an increased tax charge and would also increase your record-keeping requirements.

Because you would be deemed to have made remittances which do not accurately reflect the actual money remitted, keeping track of your foreign income and gains could become a nightmare.

One of the ways to avoid these ordering rules is to minimise the amount of nominated income which is kept segregated. You can do this by making an insufficient income nomination.

Insufficient Income Nomination

If you are subject to the £30,000 tax charge the tax legislation states that you need to make a nomination of your overseas income or gains. You need to nominate some foreign income or gains, but you do not necessarily need to nominate the full amount.

Therefore if you are a higher-rate taxpayer you would usually need to nominate around £75,000 (ignoring foreign taxes etc) to give rise to a £30,000 UK tax charge.

What if you only nominate, say, £30,000 of overseas income?

Well, in that case HMRC would deem you to have nominated an additional £45,000 of foreign income for the purposes of the £30,000 tax charge. This additional 'deemed amount' would not be actual income and could not be remitted tax free in the future.

There is a minimum 'actual' nomination of £1 meaning that you could nominate just £1 of foreign income if you wish. HMRC would then deem the income required to give rise to a £30,000 tax charge.

You could use this technique to potentially avoid the statutory ordering rules for nominated income by nominating only a small amount of foreign income which would never be returned to the UK. After all for most people it's much easier to avoid remitting £1 rather than £75,000.

So for tax year 2010/2011 you could establish a separate overseas account which would generate a small amount of income and/or gains.

You would need to ensure that the amount transferred is sufficient to ensure that at least £1 of income/gains arise in tax year 2010/2011.

You would then nominate this £1 which would be classed as an insufficient nomination and you would be deemed to have nominated income of £75,000 for the purposes of the £30,000 tax charge.

However, this £75,000 is not actual income and could not be remitted. Therefore the ordering rules above would not apply in relation to this deemed £75,000 (only to the actual £1 nominated). As such you should be able to keep this £1 overseas and remit funds from other accounts without this money being artificially classed as income.

There is some concern as to whether this limited nomination could cast doubt on the double tax relief position of the £30,000 charge under double tax treaties.

Example

Let's assume Jerry has to nominate income or gains for the purposes of the £30,000 tax charge. He has substantial overseas income and gains.

Jerry nominates £107,000 of foreign gains in Account A in year 1. This represents his nominated capital gains.

A couple of years later he remits £100,000 of these gains to the UK. If he had not remitted all his other unremitted income and gains (which would then have been taxed in the UK) this would be classed as a remittance of his nominated gains and the special ordering rules apply.

These would then deem the remittance of £100,000 to be income from his other offshore accounts even though what he actually remitted was capital gains. If, for instance, he is a high earner he could be subject to 50% income tax on the income remittances from his other accounts. This is despite the fact that he is actually remitting capital gains which may be taxed at 28%.

In order to avoid these special ordering rules Jerry would need to keep the £107,000 gain outside the UK and not remit it until all of his other income and gains have been remitted. Given that it's such a large amount of money this may be difficult (eg he may need the funds to purchase a UK property or invest in a UK business).

As an alternative to making the £107,000 nomination for Account A, Jerry could have arranged for a small amount of his investment income to be crystallised in a new account (Account B). Assuming he transferred a nominal amount of capital into this account (eg, £100) this would generate interest income in Account B of perhaps £1.

He could then nominate this £1 in Account B as his actual nominated income. Provided he retained this £1 outside the UK he would avoid the special ordering rules for nominated income. As such he could transfer the gain in Account A back to the UK which would be subject to CGT at 28%, as opposed to being deemed to be income and taxed at 50%.

Paying the £30,000 Charge

Payment of the £30,000 charge will usually be due along with the rest of your income tax or capital gains tax by 31 January following the end of the tax year (for example, 31 January 2012 for the 2010/11 tax year). Note, however, that if you nominate the £30,000 charge on overseas unremitted income, it could affect your income tax payments on account for the subsequent year.

Minimising Payments On Account

Any non-doms subject to the £30,000 tax charge will need to consider how their payments on account will be impacted. This is particularly the case where they swap and change between the remittance basis and the arising basis in different tax years.

Payments on account are simply advance payments of income tax. Each payment on account is half of the total tax bill that you had to pay directly to HMRC on your income for the previous tax year.

So if your total income tax for 2009/2010 was £10,000 the payments on account due for 2010/2011 would be as follows:

- 31 January 2011 – 1st payment on account – £5,000
- 31 July 2011 – 2nd payment on account – £5,000

How is the £30,000 Classed for Tax Purposes?

The £30,000 remittance basis charge can consist of either income tax or capital gains tax, or a mixture of the two, depending on what nominations are made by the individual.

As we've seen, when you pay the £30,000 tax charge you will need to nominate income that is classed as having suffered the £30,000 tax charge. If you nominate overseas unremitted income as having suffered the £30,000 tax charge, the £30,000 is classed as a payment of income tax.

This amount which has been nominated as income (and therefore treated as having incurred income tax) will need to be taken into account and included in the overall calculation of payments on account for the following year.

If you don't nominate enough overseas income or gains for the £30,000 tax charge there is a deemed amount added which is always treated as producing income tax. This then has a bearing on the payments on account position.

Any deemed amount nominated will automatically produce income tax and will then become part of your payment on account calculation for the following year.

Capital Gains

Capital gains tax is never included when calculating payments on account, so any of the remittance basis charge that is comprised of capital gains tax will not form any part of the following year's payments on account.

You may think this is a good reason to nominate overseas gains for the £30,000 tax charge, but it should be remembered that the nominated income/gains could potentially be remitted back to the UK free of tax in the future.

As such, given that income could be taxed at up to 50% and capital gains could be taxed at 20%, it may make more sense to nominate income to achieve the greatest tax saving.

Example

Patrick is a non UK domiciliary and is within the scope of the £30,000 tax charge.

He has an income tax liability of £100,000 for 2007/2008.

For the 2008/2009 tax year he then makes payments on account of £50,000 each on 31 January 2009 and on 31 July 2009. His tax liability for 2008/2009 is £150,000 which includes the £30,000 remittance basis charge. The remaining £120,000 is income tax on UK sources.

Patrick has nominated only £30,000 of his foreign income which led to a charge of £12,000 income tax. He also nominated £100,000 foreign chargeable gains which led to a capital gains tax charge of £18,000. Together these amounts constitute his £30,000 remittance basis charge.

Patrick's payments on account for 2009/2010 will be calculated using the £120,000 income tax paid on UK income sources in 2008/2009, plus the £12,000 income tax element of the remittance basis charge. This means that he will make payments on account of £66,000 on 31 January 2010 and on 31 July 2010 on account of liability for 2009/2010.

The key point to grasp here is that it's only the income element of the nominated amount that will be taken into account for payments on account purposes. The £18,000 nominated as capital gains tax won't feed through into the 2009/2010 payments on account.

Excluding Nominated Capital Gains from Payments on Account

If you have nominated some overseas gains for the purposes of the £30,000 tax charge you will need to complete an additional box in the residence supplementary pages.

This box is called 'Adjustments to payments on account' and must be completed if any nomination of capital gains is made. That is because capital gains tax is excluded from the computation of payments on account, and is simply payable as part of the balancing payment on 31 January following the tax year.

This box therefore identifies the amount of the nominated CGT (£18,000 in the above example) and excludes it from the following tax year's payments on account.

You won't need to complete this box if a nomination of income only has been made, as any amount nominated from income will be taken into account in computing the overall payments on account liability for the following year.

Swapping Between the Remittance and Arising Basis

If you swap between the remittance and arising basis you will be subject to the £30,000 tax charge in some years and not others.

Where the £30,000 charge is paid in the previous year on nominated income, the amount feeds through to your payments on account for the next year and would therefore increase the payments on account.

In order to prevent overpaying on income tax during the tax year (as you won't actually pay the £30,000 tax charge if you're taxed on the arising basis) you would need to make a claim to reduce payments on account on form SA 303.

Summary

In summary you only have to pay the £30,000 tax charge if:

- You are non UK domiciled
- Have lived in the UK for at least 8 of the last 10 years
- You choose the remittance basis

If you don't claim the remittance basis or haven't lived here for the 8 year period you won't have to pay the £30,000 tax charge.

Chapter 7

Who Should Claim the Remittance Basis?

So who should claim the remittance basis now that the rules have changed so much?

This answer depends on lots of different factors including:

- How long you've lived in the UK
- The amount of money in question
- Whether it's income or capital gains
- What you ultimately intend to do with the money

Remember you can make a different choice every year. You can claim the remittance basis this year and the arising basis next year.

You choose whichever method saves you the most tax.

And whatever you decide to do, remember this will not affect your overall non-domiciled status.

Income Under £2,000

If your overseas income and capital gains are less than £2,000 you have nothing to lose by using the remittance basis.

It doesn't matter how long you've been living in the UK – all that matters is that your unremitted income is less than £2,000.

If you're a higher-rate taxpayer this will let you save up to £799.60 per year in tax:

$$£1,999 \times 40\% \text{ tax} = £799.60$$

Income Between £2,000 and £8,474

If you have between £2,000 and £8,474 in income and capital gains you should consider keeping £1,999 overseas where it will be tax free.

This applies no matter how long you've lived in the UK.

That leaves income of up to £6,475. This should be brought back into the UK where you will pay tax on it.

What's so significant about £6,475? That's the amount of the income tax personal allowance which you will lose for the 2010/11 tax year if you decide to keep your money offshore and claim the remittance basis.

If your remaining overseas income is less than £6,475, you would be crazy to claim the remittance basis. You will end up paying more tax than otherwise.

Example

Gordon is a non-domiciled higher-rate taxpayer and earns £5,000 of interest from his overseas bank account. Let's say he keeps £1,999 overseas and remits the rest of his interest to the UK. His tax will be:

$$£5,000 - £1,999 = £3,001 \times 40\% \text{ tax} = £1,200$$

Let's say Gordon instead claims the remittance basis. His £5,000 can then be kept tax free offshore. But at the very least he will lose his income tax personal allowance which means he'll pay an extra £2,590 tax on his UK income:

$$£6,475 \times 40\% \text{ tax} = £2,590$$

So by claiming the remittance basis he ends up paying over twice as much tax.

If you have a mixture of income and capital gains, you are possibly better off remitting your gains because these will be covered by your annual capital gains tax exemption or, at the very worst, taxed at 28%, provided you're keeping less than £2,000 of income and gains abroad.

Summary

No matter how long you've lived in the UK, if your overseas income is between £2,000 and £8,474 you should:

- Keep £1,999 overseas where it is tax free
- Remit the rest to the UK and pay tax on it
- This will preserve your income tax personal allowance
- It's probably better to remit capital gains instead of income

Income Over £8,474

So we know that if you earn up to £8,474 per year you should not claim the remittance basis on your tax return, no matter how long you've lived in the country

You should keep just under £2,000 overseas and tax free, remit the rest and pay tax on it and preserve your personal allowance and capital gains tax exemption.

If you earn more than £8,474, whether you should claim the remittance basis depends on how long you've been UK resident.

UK Resident Less Than 8 Years

If you've been resident for less than 8 years (including the current year) you are not subject to the £30,000 charge and it often pays to claim the remittance basis if your income is more than £8,474.

Example

Stefan has been UK resident for 3 years and earns £10,000 interest per year from his overseas bank account. If he chooses to pay tax on the arising basis his total tax bill could be as high as £4,000 (assuming he's a higher rate taxpayer):

$$£10,000 \times 40\% = £4,000$$

If he claims the remittance basis he will not have to pay any tax on his interest but he will lose his personal allowance which means his UK tax bill will rise by £2,590

$$£6,475 \times 40\% = £2,590$$

Claiming the remittance basis saves him almost £1,500 in tax.

However, there are a couple of important things to watch out for.

Firstly, you lose your capital gains tax annual exemption if you claim the remittance basis. This may result in extra tax on any UK assets you have sold.

The CGT exemption can save you up to £2,828 per year in tax:

$$£10,100 \times 28\% = £2,828$$

Let's say Stefan also sold some UK shares. If he claims the remittance basis he will save £4,000 tax on his overseas interest but he will lose his personal allowance and CGT exemption which could increase his UK tax bill by £5,418:

$$£2,590 \text{ personal allowance} + £2,828 \text{ CGT exemption} = £5,418$$

So claiming the remittance basis will actually cause his tax bill to increase by £1,418!

The second thing you have to watch out for is bringing the money into the UK at a later date.

For example, if Stefan eventually decides to bring his £10,000 overseas interest into the UK he will still have to pay tax on it. However, he can't get back the personal allowance or CGT exemption he lost that year. These are lost forever. So he'll end up with the worst of both worlds.

Example Continued

Let's say Stefan decides to bring the same £10,000 of interest into the UK a couple of years later. He'll still have to pay 40% income tax, which comes to £4,000. But he won't be able to recover the personal allowance he lost when he claimed the remittance basis.

Losing his personal allowance increased his UK tax bill by £2,590 at the time. So you could say he has now paid a total of £6,590 tax on his £10,000 interest.

$$£4,000 + £2,590 = £6,590$$

In this case claiming the remittance basis has cost him dear. His overall tax rate is 66%.

Of course, if you keep your money overseas permanently then you will not face this problem. The critical question is, can you afford to tie your money up like this?

If you intend to live in the UK for many years and have large financial commitments then it may be difficult to keep your money trapped overseas permanently.

But if your overseas income is much larger than Stefan's, you probably have little to lose by claiming the remittance basis.

If the loss of your personal allowance and CGT exemption is tiny compared with the tax you will save, then claiming the remittance basis is probably the best thing to do.

UK Resident for Eight or More Years

If you've been living in the UK for 8 or more years you will have to pay the £30,000 charge if you claim the remittance basis.

It's only worth paying this charge if it's less than your normal UK income tax.

If you have overseas income of £75,000 your normal UK income tax on that money would be £30,000 if you are a higher-rate taxpayer:

$$£75,000 \times 40\% \text{ tax} = £30,000$$

So your overseas income has to be higher than this to make paying the charge worthwhile.

Also, don't forget that you will lose your income tax personal allowance which shelters the first £6,475 of your income from tax, so your income must exceed £81,475 or you will not save any money by claiming the remittance basis:

$$£75,000 + £6,475 = £81,475$$

You also lose your annual CGT exemption if you claim the remittance basis, so you'll have to factor in this cost if you've sold shares or investment property during the year.

The truth is most non-doms probably do not earn enough investment income to make paying the £30,000 charge worthwhile.

For example, if you earn, say, 4% on your offshore investments you would need over £2,036,875 of overseas assets before you even begin to generate any tax savings by claiming the remittance basis.

It's worth noting that for the 2011/12 tax year the personal allowance will increase to £7,475. This increase would need to be factored into the above calculations when considering whether to claim the remittance basis or not. The break-even point for a higher-rate taxpayer would then be £82,475, and not £81,475.

Foreign Tax

You also need to take account of overseas tax. If the overseas tax rate is higher than the UK rate it may make sense to claim the arising basis and let double tax relief eliminate the UK tax charge.

For example, if you paid 50% tax on your overseas interest, and are a UK higher-rate taxpayer, your UK tax charge at 40% would be eliminated by the overseas tax. It would then make sense to claim the arising basis because there would be no further UK tax to pay.

In practice, however, it's unlikely any overseas withholding tax will be more than 40%. It's more likely that overseas capital gains tax will be higher than in the UK, making it possibly worthwhile to stick with the arising basis when you sell shares or property.

The New Income Tax Rates From April 2010

A key change from 6 April 2010 is that there is now a new 50% additional income tax rate for anyone earning over £150,000.

So, as from 6 April 2010, we have the following tax rates for most forms of income:

- 20% tax for income within the basic-rate band.
- 40% tax for income in the higher-rate band but below the additional rate band.
- 50% tax for income above £150,000. For high-income earners this would be coupled with the loss of the personal allowance on income above £100,000.

Dividends

From April 2010 there will be three tax rates for dividends:

- Dividends within the basic rate band will be taxed at 10%.
- Dividends within the higher-rate band but below the new additional tax band will be taxed at 32.5%.
- Dividends above £150,000 will be taxed at a new income tax rate of 42.5%.

Note that these tax rates apply to *gross* dividends, so you will be able to offset the 10% tax credit when calculating the actual income tax you have to pay.

This means that the effective income tax rates on dividends will be 0%, 25% and 36.1% respectively.

The 36.1% rate is calculated as follows:

Net dividend	£90
Grossed up to	£100
Income tax at 42.5%	£42.50
Less tax credit	£10
Income tax payable	£32.50

Effective income tax rate = £32.50/£90 = 36.1%

Changes to the Personal Allowance

As from 6 April 2010 your income tax personal allowance is gradually withdrawn when your income exceeds £100,000.

Your personal allowance is reduced by £1 for every £2 over the limit (in other words, by half of the amount by which your income exceeds the limit).

So once your income reaches around £113,000 you generally won't be entitled to any UK personal allowance.

How Do the Changes Affect Non-Doms?

The above rules apply to non-doms in the same way as other UK residents. Non-doms who have taxable income above £100,000 will see their personal allowance restricted/withdrawn and anyone earning over £150,000 will need to pay the new income tax rate of 50% or 36.1% depending on the type of income.

Non-doms with overseas unremitted income should take these new rules into account when deciding whether to claim the remittance basis or the arising basis.

If for instance you will be subject to the 50% income tax rate because you have a high UK income and you have substantial overseas investment (non-dividend) income you would have a choice of either:

- Claiming the remittance basis and paying the £30,000 tax charge. You could then keep the income abroad to avoid UK tax. There would be no loss of the UK personal allowance as it would have been withdrawn anyway because you have income well in excess of £100,000.

- Opting for the arising basis and paying income tax at 50% on the overseas income.

The fact that you would now be paying UK tax at a much higher rate and that filing a claim for the remittance basis would not cause you to lose your personal allowance could affect your decision.

We have already seen that for 2010/2011 if you are a higher-rate taxpayer it may make sense to claim the remittance basis if your overseas unremitted income is above £81,475. This is because at this point the loss of the personal allowance and the saving of tax at 40% would cover the £30,000 remittance tax charge.

However, if you're paying tax at 50% there would be no loss of personal allowance to take into account. In this case if you had overseas unremitted income of £60,000 or more this may make claiming the remittance basis more attractive due to the higher rate of tax (50% x £60,000 = £30,000).

Overseas Capital Gains

If your overseas capital gains are quite small it's probably not worth claiming the remittance basis.

If your gains for the year are less than the £10,100 annual CGT exemption these could be remitted back to the UK tax free – as long as you don't have any other UK gains that have used up your exemption already. A married couple can enjoy up to £20,200 of tax-free capital gains per year.

Provided your other overseas unremitted income and gains are less than £2,000 there will be no further tax to pay.

If your overseas capital gains are slightly higher than the annual exemption it may still be better to pay tax under the standard arising basis so as to protect your income tax personal allowance.

At what point is it worth claiming the remittance basis? That depends on whether you are subject to the £30,000 charge or not.

The UK capital tax rate has seen some substantial changes over the past few years. For any disposals between 6 April 2008 and 22 June 2010 there is a fixed CGT rate of 18%. This means you may need substantial overseas gains to make claiming the remittance basis worthwhile.

However, for disposals after 22 June 2010 the rate will be 18% if you are a basic-rate taxpayer buy 28% if you are a higher-rate taxpayer. If you are subject to the 28% rate of CGT this therefore reduces the amount of overseas gains needed before a claim for the remittance basis makes sense.

If you are subject to the £30,000 charge and assuming you earn no other overseas income and are a higher-rate taxpayer, you would need a gain of more than £107,143 to make claiming the remittance basis worthwhile on disposals after 22 June 2010:

$$£107,143 \ \times \ 28\% \ CGT = £30,000$$

This ignores the loss of the annual CGT exemption that applies to anyone claiming the remittance basis. When you take this into account you would need to have an overseas unremitted capital gain of more than £117,243 (£107,143+£10,100) before claiming the remittance basis makes sense.

For disposals between 6 April 2008 and 22 June 2010 you would need to have overseas unremitted gains of at least £176,767 before claiming the remittance basis made sense.

If you are in your 7th year of UK residence you should think about realizing capital gains on your overseas assets before the £30,000 charge applies. This can be achieved by selling your assets to an unconnected third party or transferring them to a trust or to another person such as an unmarried partner or adult child. Transferring assets to your spouse will not work, however.

Foreign Capital Gains Tax

It's also worthwhile considering the foreign tax position at this point. It always amazes us how many people forget that the UK isn't the only country in the world which makes you pay tax!

If the foreign capital gains tax is more than the UK tax, it would make sense to simply claim the arising basis and let double tax relief do its job and eliminate the UK tax charge.

Example

Stefan has an overseas capital gain of £250,000 which he retains abroad. He has no other overseas income. He has been UK resident for the last 10 years and will be subject to the £30,000 charge if he claims the remittance basis. He has paid foreign tax of £70,000 on the overseas gain already.

So if he claims the remittance basis his total tax will be £100,000:

£70,000 foreign tax + £30,000 charge = £100,000

However, there will be no UK tax bill if he opts for the arising basis:

	£
Gain	250,000
Less Annual exemption:	10,100
Chargeable gain	239,900
CGT at 28%	67,172
Double tax relief	-67,172
CGT payable	NIL

In this example, it would therefore make sense to simply opt for the arising basis because there is no UK tax payable in any case. Claiming the remittance basis will result in an extra £30,000 of tax plus the loss of his UK allowances.

This would also allow Stefan to immediately remit the full proceeds free of further tax. If he opted for the remittance basis he would need to elect for the gain on which the £30,000 tax charge was based (e.g. £107,143) and any remaining gain would be taxed when the proceeds were remitted in the future.

Of course, matters are not always this simple. For example, Stefan may also have earned significant overseas income in the same tax year, which could make claiming the remittance basis worthwhile.

While it's possible to swap between the remittance and arising basis on a year by year basis, you can't choose the remittance basis for income but the arising basis for capital gains.

If the overseas income has been taxed at a relatively low rate, the remittance basis could be preferable. You have to weigh up the additional tax cost of claiming the arising basis and paying full UK tax on the overseas income versus claiming the remittance basis, paying the £30,000 tax charge but having no further tax liability.

Summary of Non-Dom Tax Benefits

- Remember there is only a requirement to pay the £30,000 tax charge where you have been UK resident for more than 7 of the previous 9 tax years.

- The remittance basis can still be used by any non-doms with unremitted income or gains of less than £2,000 without any loss of allowances or requirement to pay the £30,000 tax charge.

- As we'll see shortly there are lots of exemptions and ways you can remit overseas income and gains into the UK free of tax.

- Non-dom status also has inheritance tax advantages. Provided you haven't been UK resident for more than 17 of the previous 20 tax years and haven't made the UK your permanent home, you'll only be subject to UK inheritance tax on your UK estate.

- Crucially, and probably most important of all, non-dom status gives you choice by allowing you the option of claiming the remittance basis or opting for the arising basis.

Chapter 8

Remittance Loopholes Closed

New rules have been brought in that tighten up on when overseas income and capital gains are treated as actually being remitted to the UK.

Determining when income and gains are treated as remitted to the UK is of crucial importance.

Example

Ricardo is non-domiciled and is claiming the arising basis for the current tax year, however he has unremitted income from previous tax years of £25,000. This income hasn't been taxed yet.

If he does something with this money he has to know whether that will be treated as a remittance and taxed.

Under the old rules it was often possible to bring money into the UK without it being classed as a remittance and taxed. Essentially you were able to 'have your cake and eat it'.

The new rules introduced from 6th April 2008 have clamped down on a lot of these loopholes. Broadly speaking, the new legislation treats income or gains as remitted to the UK if two conditions are satisfied:

- Cash or other property is brought to the UK for the benefit of a 'relevant person' and

- The property that is remitted is (or is derived from) the income or capital gain.

Relevant persons include:

- You, the non-domiciled person
- Your spouse, civil partner or unmarried partner
- Your children aged under 18
- Your grandchildren aged under 18
- Certain companies and trusts that you are involved with

So the key change here is that a remittance takes place not just if you benefit but also if certain other close family members can benefit.

The new rules also clamp down on using foreign income outside the UK to satisfy a debt in respect of UK property. For example, if you borrow money overseas to buy UK property and then pay off the debt with overseas income, this will now usually be classified as a remittance.

Existing offshore mortgages for residential property will not be treated as remittances but this concession only lasts for the term of the mortgage and will be scrapped on 5th April 2028.

Note that income counts as remitted if it is received in the UK on your instructions. It therefore doesn't need to be received directly by you to be classed as a remittance.

It used to be possible to purchase moveable assets overseas such as paintings and avoid tax when the assets were brought back to the UK. This will also now be classed as a taxable remittance.

However, assets that you owned on 11 March 2008 that were purchased out of untaxed relevant foreign income will remain exempt, even if the asset is currently outside the UK and is brought into the country later on.

Credit Cards and Debit Cards

If you use a UK credit card to pay for goods or services (either in the UK or overseas) and then settle the credit card bill using overseas income or gains, the payment is a taxable remittance.

This is because using a UK credit card creates what is known as a 'relevant debt' under the new legislation.

A taxable remittance can occur when your foreign income or gains are used outside the UK to settle a relevant debt.

Broadly speaking, this provision prevents you taking an overseas loan, spending the money in the UK and then arguing that there is no tax because you used foreign income or gains to repay the foreign debt, without bringing any of your income or gains into the UK.

Overseas Credit Cards

The use of an overseas credit card to pay for goods used or received in the UK, or services provided in the UK for your benefit (or the benefit of your wife, minor children etc) will create a 'relevant debt'.

Therefore the use of your unremitted foreign income or gains to pay the credit card company will be treated as a taxable remittance.

Using Overseas Credit Cards Overseas

If you use an overseas credit card *overseas*, you can use your unremitted income and capital gains to settle the bill without creating a taxable remittance.

That part of the payment that does not relate to UK goods or services provided inside the UK will not be classed as a remittance. So you would need to apportion the interest and other charges between UK and non-UK goods and services.

In most cases a straight proportional split of the interest against the expenditure will be acceptable.

Overseas Debit Cards

Payments for goods or services using a debit card issued by an overseas bank are treated in the same way as cash transactions. They aren't classed in the same way as credit cards, as there is no 'relevant debt' created.

This means that when goods or services are purchased in the UK using an overseas debit card, a taxable remittance of overseas income or gains could be made.

Similarly any cash withdrawals from shops or cash machines in the UK are taxable remittances.

However, any payment that relates to overseas goods or services would not usually be classed as a taxable remittance.

The new remittance rules are therefore very wide although there are a few exemptions. It's worth taking a closer look at these as they can allow some significant sums to be brought into the UK without triggering a tax charge.

Chapter 9

Tax-free Remittances

In some cases money or property remitted to the UK will not be taxed:

Remittances to Pay the £30,000 Charge

If you do opt for the remittance basis and are subject to the £30,000 tax charge you can remit £30,000 to pay the annual charge without that money itself being taxed as a remittance.

This exemption will only apply to remittances that relate to the £30,000 remittance charge and are covered by the exemption. Remittances of foreign income or gains to pay any other UK tax liabilities (eg other income tax or capital gains tax) are chargeable to UK tax.

So if you have other taxable remittances and then remit some overseas income to pay the tax on the earlier remittances, the later remittances would still be taxable.

Does Payment Need to Be Made in Full?

It can be paid in one or more amounts, however the exemption is limited to £30,000.

Therefore you can pay the £30,000 in one lump sum or as part of the payments on account and it would still qualify for the exemption.

How Do You Make a Direct Remittance to HMRC?

The exemption only applies where the remittance basis charge is paid from foreign income or gains and the payment is made direct to HMRC. This can be done either by:

- A cheque (drawn on a foreign bank account)
- An electronic transfer of funds eg a CHAPS transfer

You should ensure that you retain the paperwork to support the transaction. For example, take a copy of a cheque (or cheques) drawn on the foreign bank account, or keep the relevant bank statement identifying the bank transfer.

If the sum is first paid into a non-dom's UK bank account this would be classed as a taxable remittance.

Repayments of the £30,000

If there is a repayment of the £30,000 charge by HMRC this is treated as a remittance of any foreign income or capital gains used to pay the charge that was originally exempt.

Art Exemption

This exemption will not be of interest to most non-domiciled people but it's worth noting that there is an exemption that allows art works to be brought into the UK for public display without them being taxed as a remittance.

Clothing, Footwear, Jewellery and Watches

This is a very interesting exemption. Clothing, footwear, jewellery and watches purchased out of foreign income and capital gains are exempt property if they are for personal use.

These means they can be brought into the UK and no tax will be payable.

These assets meet the personal use rule if they are the property of a 'relevant person' and are for the use of a 'relevant individual'.

A relevant person/individual includes not only the non-domiciled person but also his spouse/civil partner (or unmarried partner) and children under 18 and grandchildren aged under 18.

Example

Felix is non-domiciled and purchases five expensive watches overseas costing £5,000 each for his wife and four grandchildren (who are under 18).

There would be no tax to pay on the £25,000 remittance when he brings the watches into the UK as this would be covered by the personal use exemption.

It would not be possible to then sell these watches in the UK and escape tax, however. Property which ceases to be exempt property – for example if it's converted into cash – will also be treated as a taxable remittance.

In the original proposals this exemption only applied to assets purchased out of foreign *income*. This included interest, dividends, rental income and business income but did not include certain forms of overseas salary income or capital gains.

However, the 2009 Budget extended the scope of this exemption as from 6 April 2008. Assets purchased out of overseas capital gains and overseas employment income can now qualify.

Assets Costing Less than £1,000

Apart from the exemption for clothing, footwear, jewellery and watches, any property with a value of less than £1,000 can be brought into the UK tax free. There is no requirement that it needs to be for personal use.

Again the 2009 Budget extended the scope of this rule so that it now applies if the overseas property is purchased out of foreign income *or* capital gains.

Furthermore, 'property' means assets not cash. For example, if you bring cash of £999 into the UK you cannot take advantage of the £1,000 exemption.

There are provisions to prevent assets form being artificially split, for example, a pair of statues which would be worth considerably more as a pair than on their own.

In this case, when assessing the value of the asset you consider the value of the entire set and not just the value of the remitted asset in isolation.

Example

Paddy is non-domiciled and has overseas investment income. He uses some of the money to buy a computer from Malaysia for £900 which is then sent to the UK. This would not be classed as a remittance of the overseas investment income. He could also purchase other goods from abroad in each new tax year to take advantage of this exemption.

Provided the value is less than £1,000 AND he doesn't sell them there would be no remittance.

This exemption could save you up £400 tax (£800 for a non-domiciled couple) for each item and could make it worthwhile buying more assets from abroad.

It's also worth bearing in mind that the £1,000 exemption applies to *each item* and not the total value of items purchased in a tax year (unless the items are part of a set).

Example

Denis is a non-dom and uses his overseas income to purchase assets from an overseas supplier valued as follows:

- Pen £250
- Computer £950
- Camera £500

The total value of the items is £1,700 however, as each item cost less than £1,000 they are all treated as exempt remittances. Therefore the £1,000 exemption can prove very useful in allowing you to transfer a substantial sum back to the UK free of tax.

Repair Rule

Property isn't classed as remitted if it meets the repair rule. It meets this rule if it's brought into the UK to be repaired or restored.

Temporary Importation Rule

Property that is brought into the UK temporarily will also not be classed as remitted. To qualify it needs to be here for a total of 275 or less qualifying days. Note that those 275 days are the maximum number of days the property can ever be in the UK, not the number of days allowed each year.

Example

Jake is non-domiciled and has significant overseas investment income. He claims the remittance basis and then purchases a vintage motor car for £500,000. He can bring that car into the UK without it being a taxable remittance, provided the total time the car is in the UK is less than 275 days.

If you bring overseas property into the UK which qualifies under the repair rule or temporary importation rule and it then ceases to qualify, the asset will then be treated as a taxable remittance.

Chapter 10

Remitting Income from Previous Years

The arising basis only applies to income or gains that actually arise in a particular tax year.

If you go from claiming the remittance basis to the arising basis, your unremitted income from previous years is not automatically taxed.

Only when remitted to the UK will you be subject to UK tax.

There used to be a loophole that income couldn't be classed as remitted unless the source of that income still existed. For example, if you closed down an offshore bank account in one tax year and then remitted the interest in a later tax year the money could not be classed as a taxable remittance.

This loophole has now been closed – foreign income that is remitted will be within the remittance tax rules whether the source exists or not.

Are You Remitting Income or Capital?

Money held overseas by a non-domiciled person can take lots of different forms, including

- Capital accumulated before becoming UK resident
- Capital gains earned after becoming resident
- Income earned after becoming resident

Capital accumulated before you became UK resident can in principle be remitted tax free. Similarly savings you've accumulated in the UK can be transferred overseas and brought back in tax free.

However, if you remit overseas income or capital gains earned since becoming UK resident there could be tax consequences

Any remittances you make will be treated firstly as income, then as capital gains and only lastly as tax-free capital.

In practice, actually identifying what proportion of your overseas money is tax-free capital may prove difficult if you have been frequently reinvesting your profits.

The taxman does accept that identifying what is income, capital gains or capital can be complex and will accept a reasonable method of allocation.

It's therefore imperative that you keep good records so that you can keep track of your overseas income and gains and separate out the taxable and tax-free components

Pre-Existing Capital

As a general rule, any savings, capital or other cash that you accumulated before you became UK resident should be kept in a separate account.

The UK taxman will not look to tax this and this will be your 'pre-existing' capital and could be remitted free of tax, although any interest generated on this after you became UK resident would be taxed on the remittance basis.

Example

Michael became UK resident in June 2005. At this point he had overseas savings of £160,000 which consisted of:

- £100,000 inheritance from his aunt
- £50,000 savings
- £10,000 interest on his savings

All of this money was acquired before he was UK resident and will therefore be pre-existing capital which can be brought into the UK tax free. Any interest generated after June 2005 would however be potentially taxable income. However, as he's non-domiciled, he can claim the remittance basis.

Let's assume that his overseas assets now total £185,000. This includes the original £160,000 capital plus £25,000 of interest.

If he remits any funds to the UK he will need to look at the mixed funds rules to ascertain what he is remitting. In the case of a £50,000 remittance, £25,000 would be classed as taxable interest and £25,000 as tax-free capital.

The Mixed Fund Rules

The mixed fund rules are notoriously complex and therefore any non-doms with overseas income or gains should carefully consider whether they will be affected. It's worthwhile noting that although the provisions refer to 'mixed funds' they don't just apply to bank accounts but could also apply to any other asset that derives from foreign income or gains.

The mixed fund rules can also be important to some non-doms as they can open the door to increased HMRC disclosure. HMRC may want to ascertain the sources of the various elements of the mixed fund.

What is a Mixed Fund?

A mixed fund is any overseas fund which contains more than one type of income or gains and/or income or gains from more than one tax year.

So the mixed fund rules generally apply to a bank account (or other asset) which contains:

- More than one type of income or capital or

- Income or capital from more than one tax year.

What is the Effect of the Mixed Fund Rules?

There is a taxable remittance from a mixed fund generally where property (including money) is brought into the UK (or a service is provided in the UK) and the property identified is from the mixed fund.

Where there is a remittance from a mixed fund you need to ascertain the various elements of the mixed fund and then tax any remittance in a certain order.

The order is essentially income first, then capital gains, then capital. Note that the rules are actually more subtle than this as the order of remittances can be broken down into employment income, investment income, capital gains, and capital.

Mixed Funds and Overseas Bank Accounts

Many non-doms hold overseas bank accounts that are mixed funds.

You should note that a mixed fund doesn't arise just because a non-dom has a number of accounts with the same bank.

Provided each bank account is separate and contains only one of the separate types of income there will be no mixed fund.

Example

Bob is a non-dom who claims the remittance basis. He has three separate accounts with the same offshore bank:

- Account A into which he pays his overseas employment income.

- Account B into which he pays some inherited money (clean capital).

- Account C into which he pays some overseas investment income.

Each of these accounts is separate and would not be classed as mixed funds. Therefore provided they don't subsequently become mixed funds (eg if account B generates interest which is retained in account B), Bob can bring money into the UK from Account B and that will be accepted as being a transfer of 'clean' capital, and so will not be a taxable remittance.

Interest Generated on Offshore Bank Accounts

If a non-dom claims the remittance basis of tax any overseas interest earned will be taxed only to the extent that it is brought into the UK.

Care needs to be taken if there is 'clean capital' in an offshore account which generates interest. If the interest is credited to the offshore account this would then make it a mixed fund (as it contains capital and interest income). This means that if any cash was extracted from the account it would be classed as a remittance of the interest income first, before the tax free capital could be brought back.

If the interest had been held in a separate account this would then allow the tax free capital to be brought back to the UK, with the interest income retained overseas, avoiding a UK tax charge.

Can I Transfer Interest to a Separate Account and Avoid It Being a Mixed Fund?

If you have a capital account overseas which generates interest you may have this credited to the capital account before being immediately transferred to a separate interest account.

HMRC accepts that in these cases there should be no mixed fund. They have specifically stated:

"...Where a mixed fund such as this is created fleetingly by an operation of the banking system, HMRC will accept that the interest credit will not taint the principal and so that the mixed fund rules...do not apply..."

Capital Losses

Non-doms who claim the remittance basis are not usually entitled to relief for overseas capital losses.

Non-doms who always claim the arising basis are entitled to relief for overseas capital losses.

These provisions are complex but there is now a special election you can make to obtain relief for your overseas capital losses.

How the Foreign Capital Loss Election Works

Before 2008/2009 overseas losses of non-doms were simply not allowable.

Therefore if you had an overseas gain and an overseas loss the capital gain was subject to capital gains tax in full when it was remitted, even though you'd incurred a foreign capital loss in the same tax year.

From 2008/2009 onwards foreign losses are allowable for non-doms providing they have made a valid election under TCGA92/S16ZA and subject to certain restrictions on their use.

The most important feature of the new rules is that an election must be made for the first year in which the remittance basis is used regardless of whether there are any losses at that point. If the election is not made for the first year (2008/09 onwards) then the power to claim foreign losses is lost forever (unless you become UK domiciled).

By making the election this then allows foreign capital losses to be offset. However, there are restrictions as to how the foreign loss can be offset. Note that the new election applies to losses that arise after 5 April 2008. If you have gains that have arisen before this date you won't get relief for the losses on a subsequent remittance of the gains due to the 'no carry back rule'.

No Carry Back Rule

When you make the election this prevents any loss (not just a foreign loss) of a later year being offset against a foreign capital gain which arose in an earlier year but which is not remitted until the year of the loss or later.

This therefore effectively prevents you carrying back capital losses against capital gains which arose in a previous tax year.

Example

Alex is a non-dom and has filed a foreign capital loss election under S16ZA.

He has unremitted capital gains of £200,000 in 2010. In 2015 he incurs a foreign capital loss of £100,000.

If he remitted the £200,000 gain in 2015 he couldn't offset the foreign capital loss due to the 'no carry back rule', as the gain arose in a previous tax year.

Special Ordering Rules

There are special provisions that limit the amount of losses available for relief by applying a strict set of ordering rules to ensure that the foreign loss is offset against certain gains first.

If the election is made then foreign losses in a year are set off in the following order:

- First against remitted foreign capital gains

- Next against unremitted foreign capital gains

- Finally against UK capital gains.

So the UK capital gains will only be offset by the foreign losses after the losses have offset all the overseas capital gains.

If you have unremitted foreign gains you'll need to keep a note of the foreign capital losses offset against them so that when you do remit the gains you'll only be subject to CGT on the reduced gain.

Making the Election

There is very little detail provided by HMRC as to the nature of the election. HMRC makes a passing mention of this election on page CGN6 of the notes to the CGT pages and there is a further brief mention of this election in the guidance on capital gains for non-doms.

However, HMRC has not specified how the election should be made and therefore a letter, or statement in the additional information section of the tax return should suffice.

Capital Losses and the Arising Basis

The election only applies for the purposes of the remittance basis.

Therefore if you don't make the election you will never have the benefit of foreign losses that arise in a year for which you claim the remittance basis.

However, if you're subject to the arising basis foreign losses that arise in that year should still be available to offset against other gains.

Pros and Cons of the Election

The big advantage to the election is that it allows you to offset foreign losses against your capital gains even though you're taxed on the remittance basis.

So, rather than having foreign capital gains still charged to CGT when you remit them, if you also have foreign capital losses, you can now offset the capital losses against the gain to reduce your CGT. Great - why doesn't everybody make the election?

Well, the provisions don't give you a blanket offset for foreign capital losses against all your gains. As we've seen above, they limit the amount of losses available for relief by applying a strict set of ordering rules to ensure that the foreign loss is offset against certain gains first.

Although you can offset the foreign losses against UK gains, UK capital gains will only be offset by the foreign losses after the losses have been offset against all the overseas capital gains.

This means that if you have unremitted foreign gains you will need to keep a note of the foreign capital losses offset against them so that when you do remit the gains you'll only be subject to CGT on the reduced gain. Nevertheless this is better than not making the election because if you didn't there would be no offset for the foreign losses in the first place.

The first big disadvantage of making the election is that when you make the foreign capital loss election it applies to all losses – both UK and foreign losses.

Ordinarily a non-dom's UK losses are offset against UK gains just as for any other UK resident. So they're offset against current year UK capital gains and then carried forward to reduce future UK capital gains. By making the election your UK losses can be offset against overseas unremitted gains.

In other words, if you had UK losses and had made the election they would be subject to the same rules as above (ie they would be offset first against remitted gains, then unremitted gains).

The unremitted gains would be franked for the future. The UK losses could therefore be used against overseas gains that are not actually within the charge to CGT, and you could have other UK gains for the same tax year still chargeable as the losses have been used on the unremitted gains.

If you had not made the election the UK losses would be offset against the actual gains chargeable thus reducing the UK gains.

The operation of the loss relief rules can get very complex as you'll need to keep account of the use of the losses against gains flowing through different tax years taking account of different remittances.

The other big disadvantage to the foreign capital loss election is in terms of disclosure.

Ordinarily non-doms with overseas unremitted gains would not need to disclose these unless they were actually remitted back to the UK.

However, if you claim the capital loss, although you don't have to report the foreign gains, you do have to calculate them to establish what losses have been used. In the event of an enquiry HMRC would then be able to ask for details of the foreign gains to establish if the losses had been utilised correctly.

Chapter 11

Making Gifts to Save Tax

As we've seen, the new rules have tightened up on what is classed as a remittance and as a result many of the previous tax planning techniques will no longer work.

However, one tax-saving technique that could still be relevant is to make overseas gifts to family members.

Under the old rules a popular technique used by non-doms was to gift overseas assets to family members who then brought those assets into the UK.

The new legislation has significantly tightened up this rule.

It will class income or gains as remitted to the UK broadly if cash or other property is brought to the UK for the benefit of the non-domiciled person or any 'relevant persons'.

Relevant persons includes:

- You, the non-domiciled person
- Your spouse or civil partner
- Your partner if you're unmarried and live together as a married couple or civil partners
- Children aged under 18
- Grandchildren aged under 18

However, there are still a number of family relationships that would not be caught by the new remittance tax rules.

These include:

- Adult children
- Adult grandchildren
- Uncles
- Aunts
- Nephews
- Nieces
- Brothers
- Sisters
- Cousins
- Separated couples
- Divorced couples

In addition, close friends would not fall foul of these rules.

Example

Johnny is non-domiciled and has untaxed overseas investment income from previous years of £20,000. If he transfers £10,000 of this to his wife this would be classed as a remittance by Johnny if she subsequently brings the money into the UK.

However, there's nothing to stop Johnny from instead transferring his £10,000 to his adult children or adult grandchildren.

He could transfer the money into an overseas bank account in their name. Provided this was a gift with 'no strings attached' and the children have full legal and beneficial ownership, and Johnny and his wife do not benefit from the transfer, his children or grandchildren could then bring the £10,000 into the UK and there would be no immediate tax charge.

This could be a tax efficient way of helping his family. There would also be no capital gains tax to pay (as cash gifts are generally not subject to capital gains tax) and there would be no inheritance tax if Johnny has been UK resident for less than 17 years.

If Johnny has been UK resident for more than 17 years he will be deemed to be UK domiciled for inheritance tax purposes and the transfer would be a potentially exempt transfer for inheritance tax purposes.

However, assuming he has made no other gifts in the current or previous tax year he'll be able to use his £3,000 inheritance tax annual exemption for the current and previous tax years.

This would reduce the gift to £4,000 for inheritance tax purposes, but the remaining £4,000 would only be classed as part of his estate if he doesn't survive for seven years from the date of the transfer.

So, making genuine gifts to adult children, grandchildren or anyone else on the above list could be a useful way of tax efficiently spreading wealth around the family.

A non-dom could also consider transferring overseas cash to an overseas company or trust which could then spend the funds in the UK. In the case of a company this would be caught by the anti-avoidance provisions if the non-dom or any of his immediate family have control of it. So you'd need to use a company that was controlled by adult children or other 'exempt' family members.

Similar rules apply for trusts – if the non-dom or any of the immediate family were beneficiaries or trustees, the trust itself would be caught by the new remittance rules.

Therefore simply transferring overseas assets into a trust you set up would not avoid the remittance provisions if the gains were remitted back to the UK. You'd therefore need to use a trust that was for the benefit of excluded family members.

In summary, if you are thinking about gifting cash or other assets overseas before having them remitted to the UK, the key ideally is to ensure that the gift is not made to individuals the taxman refers to as 'relevant people' and crucially that no 'relevant people' benefit.

Some family members do not fall within this definition, such as adult children or grandchildren. Provided the caveats mentioned earlier are observed (in other words the gift is a genuine gift and is made abroad), it may then be possible to argue there is no remittance when the money or asset is brought into the UK.

Using the £2,000 Exemption

If you have adult children and grandchildren (or other relatives) who are also non-domiciled and have little or no overseas income, you could avoid the £30,000 tax charge by transferring overseas cash to them.

All non-doms who have unremitted overseas income of less than £2,000 can keep the money overseas and tax free. Provided you do not exceed this limit:

- There is no loss of the personal allowance or CGT exemption

- There is no need to pay the £30,000 annual tax charge

Example

Dietrich is non-domiciled and has been living in the UK for over 10 years. He has an overseas bank account with £250,000 which earns £15,000 interest per year. All of the money is kept abroad.

If Dietrich opts for the arising basis of tax he'll suffer a tax charge of £6,000 per year. Claiming the remittance basis would definitely not be an option because he'd have to pay the £30,000 charge.

What Dietrich could do to avoid tax in the future is transfer some of the money to his family. Let's assume he has two adult children who are also non-domiciled.

He could transfer just over £30,000 to each of them to hold in their own overseas bank accounts. As long as the interest they receive is less than £2,000 there would be no UK tax payable.

This could save Dietrich's family just under £1,600 per year in tax:

$$£1,999 \times 2 \times 40\% \text{ tax} = £1,599$$

Using Minor Children

In the 2008 Budget it was announced that the new £30,000 annual tax charge will not apply to individuals under the age of 18.

Therefore one option could be to transfer overseas assets to non-domiciled children.

The children would be treated in the same way as the non-domiciled adult, except the £30,000 tax charge will not have to be paid. The children will lose their income tax personal allowance and annual CGT exemption but the avoidance of the £30,000 tax charge could generate significant tax savings.

If the children are non-domiciled they could then claim the remittance basis and avoid UK tax by retaining income or capital gains overseas.

Note that as the children would be 'relevant people', any remittance by them would be a taxable remittance in the hands of the non-dom parent. However, this could be avoided by retaining all of the money abroad.

There are, however, a number of other issues that should be considered:

Capital Gains Tax

Any transfer of assets by the parent to the children would count as a sale for capital gains tax purposes. The parent will then either have to pay tax on this gain or claim the remittance basis and suffer the various penalties, including possibly the £30,000 charge.

The best option would probably be to transfer assets that have not risen much in value or simply transfer cash to the child and then have assets purchased in their name.

Income Tax

Although children under the age of 18 don't have to pay the £30,000 tax charge there are dangers to watch out for.

The tax legislation includes provisions to prevent people saving tax by transferring income-earning assets to minor children. These are known as the settlement rules.

Where a parent transfers assets which produce income of more than £100, the income is then treated as the parent's for tax purposes.

However, the good news is that, even if caught by this rule, it is only income that parents have to pay tax on and not capital gains.

In terms of the ownership of any overseas assets, the parent could consider using a bare trust or nominee agreement. Both allow legal title to be separated from the beneficial ownership with the latter held by the child.

Alternatively, another trusted adult could hold the legal title.

Another option could be to transfer assets to a grandchild or other child (for example, a niece or nephew). Gifts to these family members would not be caught by the settlement rules, provided the person who makes the gift and his spouse do not retain an interest in the asset transferred.

Income could then be generated offshore free of UK tax by using the remittance basis.

Chapter 12

Non-Dom Investment Strategies

Deferring Income Until You Leave the Country

Because many non-doms will have to pay a heavy price for using the remittance basis, deferring income until you leave the country and become non-resident could be an attractive strategy.

If you don't earn any income or capital gains you don't have anything to fear from either the remittance basis or the arising basis.

Also don't forget the £2,000 small income exemption. Provided any overseas investments generate less than £2,000 in income or capital gains the remittance basis can be used to retain the income overseas without it being taxed.

Ideally you'd then be looking to sell the investments after you've left the UK free of UK capital gains tax.

Offshore Bonds

One way of avoiding having any income at all is to invest in an offshore bond.

Offshore bonds generally benefit from what is known as gross roll up which essentially means your money grows tax free without any income tax or capital gains tax being payable from year to year.

It's usually only when you sell the investment that tax is payable.

These investments could be attractive to many non-doms who would otherwise have to pay the £30,000 charge. They could potentially invest in an offshore bond and opt for the arising basis.

Because no income is earned from year to year there will possibly be no UK tax liability.

Offshore investment bonds also allow tax-free withdrawals of up to 5% of your initial investment per tax year.

Although you will be taxed when you cash in the bond this may not be a problem if you have become non-resident and are no longer subject to tax in the UK.

Many non-doms have been looking at using offshore bonds as an alternative to claiming the remittance basis, which now comes with significant penalties such as the £30,000 charge and loss of allowances.

Drawbacks of Offshore Bonds

You should, however, be careful about investing in one of these products without taking professional advice. If you're UK resident when you cash in the bond you'll be subject to income tax on the gain. This means you could be taxed at 40% if you are a higher-rate taxpayer. By contrast, if you invest directly in similar investments you would probably qualify for capital gains tax treatment which means a 28% tax rate and a generous annual capital gains tax exemption.

The other potential danger of offshore bonds is that the Finance Act defines remittances very widely. So you need to be careful about investing money from an overseas bank account which contains untaxed income or gains.

The taxman uses tracing rules to trace gains through different investments. So there could be a case for arguing that any money remitted from your offshore bond constitutes a remittance of the earlier income or gain which would then be taxed.

Therefore while offshore bonds could be effective in terms of deferring income, you'll need to be careful if you used untaxed income or gains to purchase the bond.

Ensure you take detailed advice from a qualified adviser.

Pensions

Contributing to a pension, such as a self-invested personal pension or SIPP, is one of the easiest ways of reducing your income tax bill.

Pensions offer three major tax breaks:

- Tax relief on your contributions
- Tax-free investment growth
- A tax-free lump sum when you retire

Tax relief on your contributions means you get all your investments at a 40% discount if you're a higher-rate taxpayer (subject to various restrictions if you're a high earner). Your contributions can then grow without having to pay any income tax or capital gains tax.

When you retire you can take up to 25% of your savings as a tax-free lump sum.

The rest of your money generally has to stay inside the pension plan and any income you withdraw is fully taxed.

Many non-domiciled people wish to retire abroad. The critical question is how will your pension be taxed if you emigrate?

There are special tax deduction at source rules which mean that any pension paid to you is subject to UK tax before you receive it. The pension provider accounts directly to Revenue & Customs.

However, there are ways around this. Firstly, there are a number of double tax treaties that can ensure that the country you retire to has the right to tax your pension instead of the UK.

For example, The UK-Cyprus double tax treaty states that any UK pension will be taxed solely in Cyprus if you are a resident of Cyprus.

Of course, to save tax you would need to ensure that you live in a country that doesn't tax pensions heavily. Cyprus fits the bill here, as does Malta. For example, in Cyprus pensions are taxed at a special tax rate of just 5%.

Transferring Your Pension Abroad

Another thing you can do is transfer your pension fund abroad. UK residents are generally free to transfer their pension pot to another pension provider. This includes overseas pension schemes, provided the overseas scheme meets certain requirements.

In particular it must be a Qualifying Recognised Overseas Pension Scheme (QROPS).

A QROPS is generally a pension scheme set up outside the UK which is:

- Regulated as a pension scheme in the overseas country, and
- Subject to the overseas country's tax regime.

There are lots of countries' pension schemes that have received approval including Switzerland, Liechtenstein, St Lucia, Gibraltar and the Isle of Man, as well as more mainstream retirement destinations such as Spain, Australia, Canada and the USA.

If you transfer your pension to the overseas scheme you won't be subject to UK tax if you live abroad permanently. There is a five-year non residence requirement which means that UK rules can be applied until you have been abroad for five years.

The beauty of the QROPS regime is that once you've been non resident more than five years, the pension scheme is subject to the new country's rules. As well as tax advantages there may be fewer restrictions in the new country on how you can get your hands on your retirement savings.

Using a New Zealand QROPS for example it's possible to have up to 40% of the fund value released as a lump sum without any New Zealand tax. You may then be able to extract the remaining capital free of tax later on. Guernsey QROPS can also offer significant tax advantages.

In summary, pensions are extremely powerful tax shelters, especially if you plan to live abroad when you retire.

How Married Couples Can Save Tax

The new rules impose a £30,000 annual tax charge on anyone who claims the remittance basis and has been living in the UK for 8 or more of the last 10 years.

This means that married couples who are both non-doms need to undertake some careful tax planning to ensure they don't end up paying two sets of penalties:

- The loss of two personal allowances and CGT exemptions
- Two £30,000 charges

Therefore, where both spouses are higher-rate taxpayers, it will often be advisable to hold investments in one person's name only, especially where remittances are kept relatively low. This ensures that only one set of penalties is payable.

Another option would be for one spouse to opt for the remittance basis and retain their income abroad and pay the £30,000 charge. The other could then opt for the arising basis and bring all of their share of the income into the UK.

If you don't have enough overseas income to justify paying even one set of penalties it may be worth paying tax on the arising basis.

To make the most of this it may then be necessary for the spouse with the lowest income to own more of the overseas assets.

For example, if your spouse has no other income the first £6,475 of income will be tax free thanks to the income tax personal allowance. Even if both of you already earn income in the UK, you could still save tax by transferring assets to your spouse if he or she is a basic-rate taxpayer paying tax at only 20%.

Similarly, assets like shares or property could be divvied up so that both of you can use your annual CGT exemptions when you sell them.

Tax-Free Overseas Investment Portfolio

The new tax rules make it unattractive for many non-doms to claim the remittance basis, especially those who are subject to the £30,000 charge.

However, it's still possible to have a sizeable overseas investment portfolio and pay little or no tax in the UK.

For example, let's say you have an overseas investment portfolio worth £200,000.

A balanced portfolio would normally contain a mixture of:

- Cash and bonds
- Shares
- Property

You can still keep almost £50,000 in a bank account or other interest-earning assets such as bonds and not worry about the UK taxman. This assumes you earn 4% interest on your money.

As long as you have less than £2,000 of unremitted interest you will not have to pay any UK tax.

That would leave you with £150,000 to invest in other assets. Let's say you invest the remaining money equally in shares and property.

The £75,000 you invest in shares will produce both capital gains and dividend income. You can avoid capital gains tax by simply holding onto your shares until you eventually leave the UK.

Alternatively, you can sell some shares every year to take advantage of your annual CGT exemption, provided you don't also have gains from a share portfolio in the UK.

In this example, even if the portfolio grows by 13% per year these gains will still be covered by your annual CGT exemption and can be remitted tax free to the UK. Gains over this amount will be taxed at up to 28% after 22 June 2010.

Your dividend income may be taxable. If you're a basic-rate taxpayer there will be no further UK tax payable but if you're a higher-rate taxpayer the tax is just 25%, provided you own less than 10% of the shares in the overseas company.

However, this problem can be mitigated and possibly avoided altogether by investing in companies that focus on capital growth and pay very low dividends.

The final £75,000 could be used to invest in overseas property. In some countries, including many emerging market hotspots, you can buy a whole property for that amount. Alternatively you could use it as a deposit and borrow the rest.

How the property is taxed will depend on how it is used. If it's used exclusively as your personal holiday home there won't be any rental income so you won't have to worry about UK income tax.

Furthermore, second homes qualify for extremely favourable capital gains tax treatment. We'll take a closer look at these capital gains tax benefits shortly.

If the property is purely an investment then there will be income tax on any rental profits and capital gains tax when you sell.

Capital gains tax can be avoided by simply not selling your properties until you become non-resident.

However, to keep under the £2,000 exemption limit you may have to remit your rental profits and pay up to 40% tax.

One way of avoiding income tax on your rental profits is to make sure you don't earn any profits. For example, instead of buying one property outright you could buy two or three by taking out mortgages and claiming the interest as a tax deduction.

This is a more risky strategy but you'll enjoy capital growth on a bigger chunk of property. Gearing up your property investments in this way allows you to convert taxable rental income into capital gains that are partially or totally tax free.

In summary, the new rules for non-doms can be onerous but it is still possible to invest in a mixture of cash, shares and property and pay little or no UK tax from year to year.

Overseas Holiday Homes

If you sell an overseas holiday home you will usually have to pay capital gains tax.

If you have been non-domiciled for many years and claim the remittance basis you will have to pay the £30,000 charge and you will lose your income tax personal allowance and CGT exemption.

With a maximum capital gains tax rate of 28% you'll only start saving tax if you have a capital gain of more than £117,243.

However, it's worth pointing out that many non-doms have little to fear from the UK capital gains tax rules when it comes to overseas holiday homes.

This is because you can make a main residence election in favour of your second home, provided you do actually use it as a residence.

Main residences are not subject to capital gains tax thanks to the Principal Private Residence (PPR) exemption.

A main residence election must be made within two years of buying the overseas property and can be backdated so that the property is tax free from day one.

Where does this leave your UK home? It will then be subject to capital gains tax from the date your overseas home becomes your main residence. However, within a week of making the election in favour of your second home you can make a new election in favour of your UK home.

So, if you do this you sacrifice just one week of exemption on your main home in the UK but your overseas home gains three things:

- Main residence status for one week

- More importantly, main residence exemption for the last three years you own it. This is thanks to a very valuable capital gains tax rule which says that any property that has been your main residence at any time in the past is also tax free for the final three years you own it.

- Finally, you will also obtain private letting relief if you ever rent out the property. This relief is only available if the property has been your main residence at some point and is worth up to £40,000 per property (£80,000 if you are married).

In summary, you could obtain three years of exemption and possibly up to another £80,000 of relief in exchange for losing just one week of exemption on your main home!

Example

Hazel and Ollie are non-domiciled and have been living in the UK for many years.

They decide to buy an overseas holiday home and make a main residence election in favour of the property for one week. 10 years later they sell the property and their net gain is £150,000.

Claiming the remittance basis would be foolish because they'll both have to pay the £30,000 charge. Even paying the charge once wouldn't make sense.

So they opt for the arising basis. How much tax will they pay?

Because the property has been their main residence, the last three out of the 10 years are tax free (we'll ignore the extra week to keep things simple).

This means their taxable gain is just 7/10 x £150,000 = £105,000

Let's say they also rented the property out and qualify for the maximum Private Letting Relief of £40,000 per person. Their total taxable gain is now £25,000:

£105,000 - £40,000 - £40,000 = £25,000

Finally they can deduct their two annual CGT exemptions which in 10 years time will easily cover the remaining gain, ensuring that no capital gains tax is payable. In summary, they've made a profit of £150,000 on their overseas property and have not paid a penny in tax.

What's more they have not had to rely on their non-dom tax status to achieve this outcome.

Chapter 13

Becoming Non-Resident to Avoid UK Tax

A non-domiciled person will only be liable to the £30,000 tax charge if they've been UK resident for 8 or more of the last 10 tax years. Anyone with only occasional UK residence can therefore avoid the £30,000 tax charge.

For example, if you're UK resident for five years or so you could become non UK resident for five years to 'reset the non-dom clock'. When returning to the UK you'd then have a further 8 years before you'd be subject to the £30,000 tax charge.

Example

Patrick becomes UK resident in 2004/2005 and remains resident for:

2004/05
2005/06
2006/07
2007/08
2008/09

He's therefore UK resident for five years. He then leaves the UK and loses UK residence from 6 April 2009 until 6 April 2014 which includes the following tax years:

2009/10
2010/11
2011/12
2012/13
2013/14

During these periods of absence he can still visit the UK and indeed does visit the UK for periods of up to 90 days per tax year.

If you plough through the numbers it's not until 2021/2022 that he's actually been in the UK for 8 or more tax years out of the last 10 and therefore only from that point on would he be liable to pay the £30,000 tax charge - unless he opted for the arising basis of course, or leaves the UK again.

If you are in the UK for only two to three years before leaving the country for another two to three years, and carry this on over a number of tax years, you shouldn't fall within the £30,000 charge.

The periods of residence are matched with periods of non residence which effectively cancel each other out and prevent the 8 year residence period being exceeded in any 10 year period.

Residence

Even if you want to establish non UK residence status you can still spend significant periods in the UK, in particular if you can clearly show your home base is overseas. In this case you could spend up to 90 days per tax year in the UK (this includes any days you were in the UK at midnight).

This could therefore make leaving the UK and avoiding or at least postponing the £30,000 tax charge much easier.

Remember though that a 'split year' of residence is still counted as a full year of residence for this purpose.

A split year arises when you leave the UK or arrive in the UK part way through a tax year. In this case, by concession you are only subject to income tax on income that arises before your date of departure or after your date of arrival.

However, part years still count as full years when it comes to working out if you are subject to the £30,000 charge, so you should be careful with your timing to ensure you don't get caught out.

It's also worth noting that if you're subject to the £30,000 tax charge and leave part way during a tax year you'll still have to pay the full £30,000.

Remittances While Non UK Resident

What if you have substantial overseas income which hasn't been taxed because you kept it abroad and claimed the remittance basis?

We've already seen that if you remit the income in future tax years this will then be classed as a taxable remittance.

However, it will usually only be taxed if you're UK resident when you make the remittance.

Does this mean you can become non UK resident and then remit income to the UK free of tax and then become UK resident again.

Yes, but unfortunately the new legislation includes some anti-avoidance rules to limit the scope of this technique.

The provisions state that if you are non UK resident for less than five complete tax years, any remittances during those five years of income that arose before you left the UK will be classed as taxable remittances in the year you return.

So you can only use this technique if you can arrange to be non UK resident for at least five complete tax years.

Example

Rohan has overseas income of £100,000 arising in the 2010/11 tax year. He is not subject to the £30,000 tax charge and claims the remittance basis. He's flexible as to where he lives but does not want to pay tax on his £100,000.

If he leaves the UK on 4th April 2011 he is free to remit the income to the UK on 6th April 2011, however to avoid this being taxed on his return he will need to remain non-resident for five complete tax years.

This means he will not be able to become UK resident again until 6th April 2016. His £100,000 would then be free of UK tax.

Non Residency and Future Income

It's worth noting that the five year anti-avoidance rule only applies to income that arises in the year of departure or previous tax years.

So if you know you're going to have substantial overseas income arising in a particular year you could become non UK resident for that year and bring the income into the UK whenever you please, free of UK tax.

Overseas income earned while non-resident is free of UK tax, and the five year anti-avoidance rule does not apply.

If in the example above Rohan knew that the £100,000 was to arise in 2011/12 instead of 2010/11, he could arrange to be non UK resident for 2011/12 and remit the £100,000 to the UK whenever he wanted without having to remain abroad for five tax years.

Timing When Arriving in the UK or Leaving

Most people arriving in or leaving the UK will be looking to claim the benefit of the split-year basis. This means that:

- Non-doms leaving the UK would only be UK resident up until their date of departure, and

- Non-doms coming to the UK will only be UK resident as from their date of arrival.

The split-year basis isn't set out in the legislation but is given by virtue of Extra Statutory Concession (ESC) A11.

The key benefit of being treated under the concession as opposed to under the general rules is that you can be non-resident for a specific part of the tax year. The main advantage is that foreign income is then free of UK income tax for the non-resident part of the tax year.

Any non-doms who are leaving the UK (or arriving in the UK) may want to take advantage of the £2,000 exemption.

This ensures that provided unremitted income or gains are less than £2,000 there is no loss of UK allowances or requirement to pay the £30,000 tax charge.

However, when considering whether the 'below £2,000 threshold' limit applies the level of unremitted foreign income and gains for the entire tax year must be taken into account.

So just because you left the UK and your income after you left was free of UK tax this would not mean it wouldn't be included when assessing whether you had £2,000 of unremitted income.

Similarly if you arrive in the UK, your overseas income before you were UK resident, although free of UK tax, would be taken into account when looking at whether you had exceeded the £2,000 level.

Example

Patrick arrives in the UK on 17 October 2010 and he is resident for the tax year 2010/2011. He claims split-year treatment under ESC A11.

He has overseas interest of £2,400 for the period 6 April to 16 October 2010. He also has bank interest of £1,100 arising between 17 October 2010 and 5 April 2011. He remits £1,000 to the UK in that year.

At the end of the year his total unremitted foreign income is £2,500. Even though he has claimed split-year treatment for 2010/2011, he still has to include any foreign income that arose before he entered the UK.

In this case Patrick could remit the £2,400 free of UK income tax, given this arose before he was UK resident. However, it's likely this would be classed as a mixed fund. As such he'd be classed as remitting the £1,100 taxable bank interest before the £2,400 tax free 'capital'.

Capital Gains

Similar principles apply to the capital gains of any non-doms coming to or leaving the UK. In order to claim the £2,000 exemption unremitted gains must be less than £2,000.

However the relevant ESC (D2) states that an:

"...individual arriving in the UK who has not been resident or ordinarily resident in the UK for five years before the year of arrival is not chargeable on capital gains made between the start of that tax year and their date of arrival..

"... An individual leaving the UK who was not resident and not ordinarily resident in the UK for at least four out of seven years before the year of departure is not chargeable on capital gains made between the date of departure and the following 5 April..."

However, just as for income tax purposes, you still need to include capital gains that arise in the 'non-resident' part of any split year when looking at the £2,000 exemption.

£30,000 Tax Charge

When looking at the £30,000 tax charge you include any year of departure or arrival as a complete tax year.

The £30,000 tax charge only applies to UK residents who have been resident for at least 7 of the last 9 tax years. Therefore this means that:

- When assessing the number of tax years you've been in the UK for the £30,000 tax charge, you include any tax years you were UK resident for part of the year. So if you arrived in the UK part of the way through a tax year you would still include it.

- Similarly the £30,000 charge isn't split even if you leave the UK part of the way through a tax year and claim the remittance basis.

So if you are liable for the £30,000 tax charge and have substantial overseas investment income you may well claim the remittance basis. If you left the UK half way through the tax year to move abroad you would still be subject to the full £30,000 tax charge.

Chapter 14

The Tax Benefits of Being UK Domiciled

A question some people ask is whether it pays to be UK domiciled instead of non-domiciled.

For income tax and capital gains tax purposes the answer is No.

If you're non-domiciled you don't have to claim the remittance basis if you don't want to. You can pay tax on the arising basis, just like UK domiciled people do.

However, the difference is you can make a different choice every year. UK domiciled people cannot. Having more choice is always a good thing.

If you've been living in the UK for at least 17 tax years, you're already deemed to be UK domiciled for inheritance tax purposes, so again there's nothing to be gained from abandoning your overseas domicile.

However, if you've been in the UK for less than 17 years you may be better off losing your overseas domicile in certain circumstances for inheritance tax purposes.

You can acquire a UK domicile of choice by arguing that you have made the UK your permanent and indefinite home and, provided the facts support this, the taxman is likely to accept your wish.

The Benefit of Being UK Domiciled

So why can it pay to be UK domiciled for inheritance tax purposes?

If you are non UK domiciled and you have a UK domiciled spouse, the usual rules relating to transfers between spouses do not apply.

Spouses who are both UK domiciled can transfer assets to each other with no inheritance tax consequences.

But for transfers from a UK domiciled spouse to a non UK domiciled spouse this exemption is restricted to £55,000. Any amount above this is treated as a potentially exempt transfer (PET).

If the UK domiciled spouse dies within seven years of making the transfer, the amount will then be included in his or her estate for inheritance tax purposes.

It should be noted, however, that the usual inheritance tax reliefs and exemptions are still available. So for transfers in excess of £55,000 the nil rate band is available in the usual way. This means a total of £380,000 (£325,000 + £55,000) can be transferred to a foreign domiciled spouse before any inheritance tax becomes payable.

In addition, if the spouse making the transfer survives for seven years there will be no inheritance tax consequences.

Example

John and Jenna are married and are both UK domiciled. They can therefore transfer assets to each other without any inheritance tax consequences. So if John transfers, say, £1 million to Jenna and dies the next day, the £1 million transfer will not be taxed.

But, if Jenna was non-domiciled, only £55,000 of this would be automatically exempt, and the remaining £945,000 would be a 'potentially exempt transfer' (PET). This means it would only be excluded from John's estate if he survived for seven years.

Note that the £55,000 restriction only applies to transfers from a UK domiciled spouse to a non-domiciled spouse.

Any transfers from a non-domiciled spouse to a UK domiciled spouse would be covered by the general exemption for spouses.

To avoid this problem you could argue that you have acquired a UK domicile of choice. This means you have decided to make the UK your permanent home and intend to remain here indefinitely.

The downside of this is that the non-domiciled spouse's overseas assets would then fall within the UK inheritance tax net.

There would be nothing to prevent you leaving the UK in the future if your intention subsequently changes and you move abroad. You would then lose your UK domicile of choice and your previous domicile of origin would reassert itself.

For inheritance tax purposes, three years after you lose a UK domicile you would be deemed non UK domiciled and your overseas assets would then be outside the scope of inheritance tax.

Claiming a UK domicile could therefore in certain circumstances be beneficial, especially if transfers of UK assets need to be made to a spouse and the seven year survivorship period is unlikely to be met.

How Does the £55,000 Exemption Operate with PETs?

The £55,000 limit applies to the total of all transfers to a spouse or civil partner domiciled outside the UK. It's important to point out that it's a *lifetime limit*.

Usually a potentially exempt transfer falls out of your estate once you have survived for 7 years but this is not the case with respect to the £55,000 exemption.

Example

In June 2000 Barry, a UK domiciliary, gifted £250,000 to his wife Betty, a non UK domiciliary. £55,000 of this transfer will be exempt as the transfer is between a spouse who is UK domiciled and a non-dom spouse. The remaining £195,000 is a potentially exempt transfer (PET).

Barry dies in 2010 and leaves all of his estate to Betty who is still non-UK domiciled.

The gift of £250,000 would therefore fall outside Barry's estate as he survived for 7 years after making the transfer to Betty. However, he won't have another £55,000 exemption to offset against any other assets he leaves to Betty as the £55,000 exemption has already been used and is not available again on his death.

However, as noted earlier, the £325,000 nil rate band would still be available in the usual way.

Change to One Spouse's Domicile Status

You should also bear in mind that the £55,000 exemption is restricted if there have previously been tax free transfers due to the spouses both being non UK domiciled.

This will mainly be an issue if there is a change in status of one spouse from being non UK domiciled to UK domiciled. This is best shown by way of an example:

Example

In 2000 Barry transfers a UK property worth £400,000 to Betty. At this point they are both non UK domiciled due to both having an overseas domicile of origin and no UK domicile of choice. The value of the property transferred is free of inheritance tax as the transfer is between non UK domiciled spouses. In 2008 Barry is deemed to be domiciled in the UK and in 2010 gives £250,000 to Betty who is still a non UK domiciliary.

Although Barry is a UK domiciliary and Betty is a non-dom the £55,000 exemption is not available against the later transfer to Betty as the amount of the exemption already given under the inter-spouse transfer exemption exceeds £55,000.

It's worthwhile bearing in mind exactly which spouse will own which assets and whether any previous transfers have been made, particularly if there has also been (or will be) a change in non-dom status.

Chapter 15

Non-Dom Salaries

Many foreign nationals come to the UK to work – what impact will the new remittance tax rules have on such people's earnings?

Well in most cases the new rules will have no added impact. If they perform their duties of employment in the UK they will be subject to UK income tax on their earnings.

The same is true for all UK residents, even those who perform some of their duties overseas.

There is, however, one exception. Where an employee:

- Is UK resident and ordinarily resident
- Non UK domiciled
- Works for a foreign employer and
- Performs all duties outside of the UK

the overseas salary can then qualify for the remittance basis.

These are pretty strict requirements as not only do you need to work for a foreign employer (which is defined as a non-resident employer) you would also need to perform all of your duties overseas (aside from any 'incidental' UK duties).

This has led to the practice of split contracts, where the employment is effectively divided into two, with the UK duties being subject to one contract of employment, and the overseas duties being subject to another. This then allows the overseas contract to solely cover overseas duties to allow the remittance basis to be claimed.

Revenue and Customs scrutinize arrangements like this very closely for evidence of a genuinely separate overseas employment with the salary apportioned on an arm's length basis between the two employments.

Even if the remittance basis could in principle apply, as you work for a non-resident employer and carry out your duties overseas, after 6th April 2008 you would still be subject to the new remittance tax rules.

This means that on first arriving in the UK a non-dom employee could claim the remittance basis and avoid UK income tax on the overseas employment income. The only drawback in most cases would be the loss of the UK personal allowance and capital gains tax exemption.

If they remain here for more than seven tax years they would then need to consider whether to continue claiming the remittance basis or not. Unless the overseas employment income (together with the non-dom's other overseas unremitted income) is more than around £81,500 it would not be worthwhile claiming the remittance basis and paying the £30,000 annual tax charge.

Instead they'd be better off simply being taxed on the arising basis and being subject to normal rates of UK income tax on their earnings.

Chapter 16

Tax Benefits of Offshore Trusts

Offshore trusts can be used by non-doms to reduce UK taxes, especially when investing in foreign property.

This will only work if the trust is non-resident.

From April 6th 2008, a trust will only be non-resident if either:

- All the trustees are non-resident, or
- If only some of the trustees are non-resident and the settlor was non-UK domiciled and non-resident when the trust was set up.

The settlor is essentially the person who decides to set up the trust.

So if a settlor is UK resident it's essential that the trustees are all non UK resident.

Tax Benefits of Non-Resident Trusts

Non-resident trusts offer three potential tax benefits:

- The trust is not usually subject to capital gains tax in respect of UK or overseas assets.

    Subject to any anti-avoidance rules being applied, offshore trusts are therefore capable of sheltering both UK and foreign capital gains.

- Non resident trusts are not subject to UK tax on overseas income so, in the absence of anti-avoidance rules being applied, offshore trusts can also shelter any rental income derived from foreign property.

  Note, however, that the trust would be subject to income tax if the source of the income is in the UK (just as an individual would be).

- If a non-domiciled individual establishes a trust, the property in the trust becomes 'excluded property' which means it is not subject to inheritance tax provided:

  o The settlor was not UK domiciled (or deemed domiciled) at the time the trust was established, and
  o The trust property is situated outside the UK.

In summary, using an offshore trust could be an attractive way for a non-domiciled person to hold overseas assets such as property as it may be possible to avoid income tax, capital gains tax and inheritance tax.

However, thanks to new anti-avoidance rules, whether a non-dom can use an offshore trust to avoid UK taxes depends on whether they are taxed on the remittance basis or the arising basis.

Anti-Avoidance Legislation

Just because a trust is non resident doesn't mean it can always be used to save tax. The taxman has a number of anti-avoidance rules at his disposal.

These include:

- The transfer of assets abroad rules
- The 'settlor' rules
- The 'beneficiary' rules

Each of these is a complex piece of legislation which means it's essential to get professional advice before you do any tax planning using offshore companies and trusts.

These anti-avoidance rules can be used to make a UK resident who establishes a trust or a UK resident beneficiary pay tax on the trust's income and capital gains.

The tax treatment of a non-dom who sets up or benefits from an offshore trust will depend on whether they are taxed under the:

- Remittance basis (or are automatically entitled to it due to having overseas unremitted income of less than £2,000), or the

- Arising basis

Remittance Basis

From April 2008 there are special tax rules for non-doms who benefit from offshore trusts.

The UK resident settlor can be taxed on the trust's income if any of it is brought back into the UK.

The capital gains rules are different. A non-dom who establishes an offshore trust won't have to pay capital gains tax, unless he or she is also a beneficiary of the trust.

UK domiciled people are taxed completely differently. They pay tax on the income and gains of the trust, whether the money is brought into the UK or not.

However, this special tax treatment for non-doms only applies if the non-dom:

- Actually claims the remittance basis, or

- Doesn't claim it but is entitled to use it anyway due to having overseas unremitted income and gains of less than £2,000.

Unless the remittance basis is used, any non-dom settlors and beneficiaries of trusts would be taxed on the trust income and gains anyway (whether they keep the trust income and gains abroad or not) if they benefit from the trust.

Summary – Taxation of Remittance Basis Users

If you set up an offshore trust and claim the remittance basis:

- You'll be taxed on the remittance basis on any overseas income the trust earns if you can benefit from the offshore trust.

- You'll be taxed on the remittance basis for any capital gains of the trust if you receive money or benefits from the trust.

Example

Peter is non-domiciled and forms an offshore trust into which he transfers overseas property assets. The trust retains all income abroad.

Peter and his wife (who is also non-domiciled) claim the remittance basis as they have substantial overseas income and don't have to pay the £30,000 tax charge (as they've been in the UK for less than 8 years).

Any income of the trust should be exempt from UK income tax and any gains would also be exempt from UK CGT if the trust is non resident.

Peter and his wife should not be subject to tax on the income or gains of the trust as the income is retained abroad and they aren't trust beneficiaries.

By contrast if Peter and his wife were UK domiciled the income of the trust would be taxed on him as would any capital gains.

Offshore Trusts and the £30,000 Tax Charge

The tax legislation makes it clear that non-doms will only be able to take advantage of this special tax treatment for offshore trusts where they are subject to the remittance basis.

This raises the spectre of the dreaded £30,000 charge if the settlor or beneficiary has been UK resident for more than seven tax years.

In terms of inheritance tax, the new rules change nothing and an offshore non resident trust can still be an excluded property trust and outside the scope of UK inheritance tax.

Offshore Trusts and the Arising Basis

If a non-dom is taxed on the arising basis they will be taxed in the same way as individuals who are UK resident and UK domiciled. This means they'll potentially have to pay tax on the income and capital gains of the offshore trust.

However all is not lost!

We've already stated that, unlike the income tax rules, you won't be taxed on capital gains that the trust makes just because you set up the trust (as non UK domiciliaries are exempt from this provision – even if they are taxed on the arising basis).

You usually need to actually be a beneficiary of the trust before capital gains are taxed on you. There are therefore two ways that the trust could be used to avoid CGT.

Firstly you could simply avoid being a beneficiary. This is where grandchildren's settlements are popular.

You could establish an offshore trust for the benefit of grandchildren and this would still be an effective shelter of foreign income and foreign gains for a non-domiciliary. Common assets for the trust to hold would be either shares in a non-resident trading company or a portfolio invested abroad for income.

Secondly you could be a beneficiary but avoid any receipts or benefits from the trust.

If you're a beneficiary of an offshore trust there are special rules that can apply so that capital gains of the trust are taxed in your hands. However, you'll only be taxed on the capital gains when you receive a 'capital payment' from the trust.

The rules define capital payment very widely. It includes

- The transfer of an asset, for example company shares

- The conferring of any benefit. This is a broad term and includes, for example, rent-free occupation of trust property.

If you receive a benefit from an offshore trust the anti-avoidance rules can result in you paying tax on this benefit if the trust has made previous capital gains. There are complex 'matching rules' to match the capital gains of the trust with the capital payments.

However, as the capital gains of the trust would only be taxed if you received a capital payment, a simple way for non-doms to realise capital gains tax free in an offshore trust is to ensure that they don't receive any capital payments from the trust.

No gains would then be taxed in the non-doms' hands while UK resident (as there are no capital payments) and if the non-dom then leaves the UK in the future he or she could access the trust capital free of UK tax. This is a potentially attractive use of an offshore trust.

Using Offshore Trusts for UK Assets

There is no difference in the capital gains tax treatment if the assets of the trust are UK or overseas assets. In both cases a UK resident non-dom would only be taxed on gains of the trust if they are subject to the remittance basis and receive benefits from the trust in the UK.

So for CGT purposes the trust could equally hold UK or overseas property and benefit from the CGT exemption if the trust settlor wasn't a trust beneficiary (or didn't receive capital payments from the trust).

If the non-dom settlor was taxed on the arising basis, the gains of the trust would be taxed in their hands if they received any capital payments (whether in the UK or overseas).

However, in terms of income tax, any UK source income produced by the trust will be taxed in the hands of the non-dom settlor as it arises if he can benefit from the trust income.

Any UK property held by an offshore trust would also not be excluded property for inheritance tax purposes and therefore there could be inheritance tax implications for the trust.

Chapter 17

Tax Benefits of Offshore Companies

The other option for any non-doms interested in holding assets offshore would be to use an offshore company.

The main advantage in using an offshore, non-UK resident company is that it's exempt from UK corporation tax on overseas income and capital gains. It's therefore very useful for holding overseas property or carrying out an overseas trade.

The problem with using an offshore company, just like an offshore trust, is the anti-avoidance rules.

The UK taxman knows just how effective offshore companies could be in avoiding UK tax, so they have brought in strict rules that restrict the tax benefits available.

Anti-Avoidance Rules

The main anti avoidance rules that apply to using an offshore company are:

- Company residence

- Apportionment of gains

- Transfer of assets abroad legislation

Company Residence

The offshore company will be classed as UK resident if its management and control are in the UK. This would defeat the whole purpose of having the company as it would then be subject to UK corporation tax on its worldwide income and capital gains.

If the shareholders are UK resident the only way you can argue that the company is non resident is by appointing an independent overseas board of directors. Revenue & Customs will then want to know:

- Do the directors of the company truly exercise management and control?

- Where do they exercise it?

- If not the directors, who exercises it and where?

Revenue and Customs has made it clear they will look at offshore companies to see if control is actually exercised from abroad or whether it is just a sham. Having overseas directors merely rubber stamping instructions from you in the UK will not work.

In order to establish the company as non-UK resident:

- All or, at the very least, most of the directors should be based outside the UK.

- The non-UK directors should be active in making business decisions.

- All major policy decisions should be decided in board meetings outside the UK (for example, purchasing and selling any property, or issuing instructions to any managing agents in the UK).

- Any agreements should be concluded outside the UK.

So a non-domiciled UK resident can establish a non-resident company but you would need to effectively sit back as the shareholder and appoint non resident directors to decide matters and run the company.

Revenue & Customs may still take a close look at such arrangements to ensure that you don't involve yourself in executive decisions, especially if the company is an investment company.

If you can't avoid the company being controlled from the UK you won't stand any chance of getting income or capital gains tax benefits from your offshore company.

Apportionment of Capital Gains

Even if you do establish the company as non resident the taxman may make you pay tax on any capital gains the company makes.

Revenue & Customs have introduced new rules which apply from April 2008 which state that if a shareholder is:

- UK resident but non UK domiciled, and
- Subject to the remittance basis of tax

the offshore company's capital gains are only taxed in the shareholder's hands when remitted.

So if you're claiming the remittance basis (which would then raise the spectre of the £30,000 annual charge and the loss of allowances) or are automatically entitled to it (because your unremitted income and gains are less than £2,000) any capital gain made by the offshore company would be free of tax provided the proceeds are kept abroad.

If you're not subject to the remittance basis because you pay tax on the arising basis, you'll pay tax on the company's capital gains, whether or not you retain the proceeds abroad. This only applies if you held more than 10% of the company's shares.

Offshore Companies and Income

What about the offshore company's income?

Unfortunately there are specific rules known as the 'transfer of asset provisions' that can apportion the company's income to the UK shareholders. These rules apply where an individual is UK resident, transfers assets to an offshore company and can then benefit from any income that arises.

Where these conditions are fulfilled, the income which becomes payable to the offshore company is deemed to be that of the individual.

There are, however, two key exceptions:

- Firstly there is a motive exemption. Under this you would essentially need to argue that the purpose of the transfer was not to avoid tax, and that it was a bona fide commercial transaction.

- If you're claiming the remittance basis any income of the overseas company is only taxed in your hands if you bring it into the UK.

So a non-domiciled person can benefit from the remittance basis by using an offshore company although this may come at a price, for example paying the £30,000 tax charge.

Summary – Offshore Company Tax Benefits

So who can actually benefit from using an offshore company? Here are some examples:

- Individuals who make sure the company is controlled overseas. If you can't do this the offshore company will be fully subject to UK corporation tax.

- Anyone who holds less than 10% of the shares in the company will be able to use it to avoid capital gains tax. If you own less than 10% you're exempt from the provisions which make shareholders pay tax on an offshore company's gains.

- Anyone with a sound commercial reason for using the offshore company will possibly be able to use the company to avoid UK tax on income.

- Any non-doms who retain income or capital gains overseas and are claiming the remittance basis. This includes:
    - Individuals not liable for the £30,000 charge (for example, those UK resident for less than 8 tax years).
    - Those already paying the £30,000 charge because they have substantial other overseas income or gains.
    - Those who generate substantial income from the offshore company. This would then make paying the £30,000 tax charge and retaining the company income abroad worthwhile.

- Those thinking about becoming non-resident and wanting to avoid capital gains tax. An offshore company could be used because non-residents are excluded from the anti-avoidance rules attributing capital gains of offshore companies.

Finally, and I can't stress this enough – make sure that you take detailed advice from a tax professional before you do anything related to your non-domiciled tax status. This is a complex area and there are lots of factors to consider.

Chapter 18

Foreign Currency Bank Accounts

There have been a lot of changes in the HMRC guidance relating to foreign currency bank accounts during 2009 and 2010.

A withdrawal from a foreign currency bank account constitutes a disposal of an asset and a capital gain or loss would generally be calculated.

Withdrawals include transfers of funds into other accounts, even if that other account is denominated in the same foreign currency.

Non-doms claiming the remittance basis would be taxed if there is a remittance back to the UK.

Therefore even if you transfer forex from a US dollar account in the United States to a US dollar account in the UK this would in principle be a disposal for capital gains tax purposes.

There is a statement of practice (SP10/84) that allows UK residents to disregard direct transfers between accounts in the same currency for capital gains tax purposes.

However, SP10/84 has not historically been available to individuals who are not domiciled in the UK in respect of their foreign currency bank accounts located outside the UK.

As such, transfers by non-doms between different foreign currency accounts could potentially be subject to capital gains tax.

Extension of SP 10/84

HMRC has now introduced guidance to extend the application of SP 10/84 to non-doms in respect of transfers on or after 6 April 2008.

HMRC has said:

"...HMRC has long recognised the implications of these rules for individuals who hold foreign currency bank accounts ('FCBAs'). The effect of SP10/84 is to relieve them of the need to carry out numerous computations, but it did not apply to the offshore FCBAs of individuals who were not domiciled in the UK. This was because of the difference in treatment, for non-domiciled individuals, between accounts outside the UK, on which gains were liable to CGT only when they were remitted to the UK, and accounts within the UK, on which gains were liable to CGT when they arose.

After receiving representations from stakeholders on the effects, in this context, of the revised remittance basis of taxation introduced by Finance Act 2008, HMRC has reached the view that it is consistent with the practice described in SP10/84 to allow individuals not domiciled in the UK to treat all their FCBAs located outside the UK in a particular currency as a single account..."

Therefore, as from April 2008, non-doms can treat overseas accounts containing the same foreign currency as one account. This applies whether they're taxed on the arising basis or the remittance basis.

The result of this is that transfers between the overseas accounts would not give rise to a capital gain for capital gains tax purposes.

Note if you converted the currency into a different currency or transferred it back to the UK this could still result in the gain crystallising.

When the New Provisions Apply

HMRC states that an individual who is not domiciled in the UK can treat all bank accounts which are:

- In his name
- In a particular foreign currency
- Not situated in the UK

as one account and disregard direct transfers among such accounts for capital gains tax purposes.

If you use this practice you must also apply it to all future direct transfers among the bank accounts in your name containing that particular currency.

Therefore the capital gains tax free transfers only apply to overseas foreign currency accounts. If you transferred foreign currency into a UK account (even if it was the same currency) this would be a disposal for CGT purposes.

There is also a de minimis limit of £500 so that where your gains from transfers from overseas non-sterling bank accounts which you remit to the UK are less than £500 in any tax year, you won't have to declare these gains to HMRC.

Restriction of Losses on Forex

HMRC has also announced details of new provisions to be introduced to prevent capital losses being crystallised on foreign currency conversions in certain limited circumstances.

The rules are targeted at non-doms taxed on foreign income on the remittance basis, and apply where they are subject to income tax on a remittance of income, and there is also a capital loss on the conversion of the currency.

Where Do the New Rules Apply?

As a foreign currency bank account is an asset within the scope of capital gains tax, a withdrawal of funds from a foreign currency account constitutes a disposal (or part-disposal) of the account on which a capital gain or loss arises. The proceeds from the disposal are effectively equal to the sterling value of the amount withdrawn.

Where:

- a non-domiciled individual is taxable on the remittance basis in respect of their foreign income and capital gains,

- the individual withdraws funds from a foreign currency bank account, and

- the whole or part of the amount withdrawn represents foreign income taxable on the remittance basis,

the foreign income transferred back to the UK will be liable to income tax at the time of remittance. The amount on which income tax is due is the sterling value of the income at the time it is remitted.

However, the withdrawal of funds also represents proceeds of the disposal of the whole or part of the foreign currency for CGT purposes.

Given that an amount is not permitted to be both subject to income tax and CGT, HMRC accepts that specific tax provisions apply to exclude from the calculation of the capital gain or loss arising on disposal (or part-disposal) the part of the withdrawal that is taxable as remitted income.

130

Example

Terry is a non-dom and has foreign investment income of $20,000. Let's say this is equivalent to £10,000. He claims the remittance basis and retains the money abroad.

A couple of years later he remits the $20,000 back to the UK and this is then equivalent to £15,000.

For income tax purposes the taxable amount is £15,000.

For CGT purposes the computation is as follows:

Proceeds	£15,000
Less: Exclusion for taxable income	(£15,000)
Less: Acquisition cost	(£10,000)
Capital Loss	£10,000

Before 16 December 2009 this would have been an allowable capital loss.

However, HMRC now treats this as an 'uncommercial loss' as it doesn't reflect the true facts (i.e., Terry has incurred no real loss in these circumstances). It arises because the CGT rules adjust the consideration for the disposal, but there is no requirement to remove the relevant income element from the allowable cost.

New Rules

For disposals on or after 16 December 2009, where the disposal is a withdrawal of funds from a foreign currency bank account that includes an amount that is liable to tax as remitted income, the gain or loss arising will be calculated using special rules.

Essentially the part that is taxable as remitted income is excluded from the disposal proceeds, however any capital loss won't be an allowable loss.

In addition, the new rules will also reduce not only the proceeds but also the CGT cost of the foreign currency in proportion to the amounts withdrawn and retained.

It will only affect conversions after 16 December 2009, and therefore a loss could still arise on disposals prior to this date.

The new rules will only effect income that is taxed on the remittance basis and where there's a change in the sterling value prior to the remittance.

Therefore for this to apply you would be looking at a case where the remittance basis applied (either claimed post April 2008 or used before April 2008) and the cash was retained abroad before being remitted back to the UK.

Chapter 19

Frequently Asked Questions

Will I have to pay the £30,000 tax charge?

Not necessarily. This is not a charge on non-domicile status but rather a minimum tax charge on non UK domiciliaries where they have overseas income and gains that aren't brought back to the UK.

You'll only have to pay the £30,000 tax charge if you're:

- a non UK domiciliary who has lived in the UK for more than 7 of the last 10 tax years
- and who claims the remittance basis.

If you don't claim the remittance basis or haven't lived here for the 7 year period you won't have to pay the £30,000 tax charge.

It's also worthwhile noting that anyone aged under 18 won't have to pay the £30,000 tax charge.

Where you do pay the £30,000 tax charge you'll need to elect the overseas income or gains on which it is based and this can then be remitted in the future free of UK tax (once any untaxed income or gains have been remitted).

If I want to use the remittance basis will I always have to claim it?

Usually yes. It's only if you have unremitted overseas income or gains of less than £2,000 that no 'claim' will be necessary. In this case the remittance basis will apply automatically and the income/gains of less than £2,000 could be retained overseas free of UK tax without suffering the £30,000 annual charge or the loss of UK allowances.

It's important, however, to distinguish between the tax legislation and the tax return. The tax legislation makes it clear that non-doms with unremitted income or gains of less than £2,000 do not need to claim the remittance basis.

However the tax return requires all non-doms who wish to use the remittance to tick box 27 of the remittance pages which refers to 'claiming' the remittance basis. The difference in terminology can be confusing however when the tax return refers to 'non-doms wishing the claim the remittance basis' it actually means 'non-doms wishing to use the remittance basis'.

Therefore you will still need to tick box 27 of the remittance pages to use the remittance basis. You would then tick box 28 to ensure that there was no loss of allowances.

The 2009 Budget also extended these provisions to ensure that the remittance basis applies automatically where a non dom has total UK income or gains of no more than £100 which has been taxed in the UK, provided they make no remittances to the UK in that tax year.

How will I claim the remittance basis?

If you do want to claim the remittance basis of tax you will tick box 27 on the remittance pages of the tax return.

Will I always lose my personal allowance/annual exemption?

If you claim the remittance basis you will usually lose the personal allowance (including the blind person's allowance) and the CGT annual exemption.

There is an exception to this where the remittance basis applies automatically (eg where unremitted overseas income or gains are less than £2,000). In this case the allowances will not be lost.

Does the loss of the annual exemption only apply to overseas gains?

If you do claim the remittance basis and lose the annual exemption it will not be available for offset against UK or overseas gains.

I have overseas income - should I claim the remittance basis or not?

Generally speaking if you are subject to the new £30,000 tax charge, are a higher rate taxpayer and the overseas unremitted income is less than around £81,475 it may be worthwhile sticking with the arising basis. In this case the UK tax on the overseas income (less the tax saving from being able to use the UK personal allowance) will be less than the minimum £30,000 tax charge payable if you claimed the remittance basis.

Can I still avoid remitting income by gifting cash to family overseas?

The legislation has clamped down on this practice. In the past it used to be possible to gift cash to family members overseas who would then bring the cash into the UK.

The new legislation looks to class this as a remittance if the transfer into the UK was by or for the benefit of you or any 'relevant people'.

The definition of relevant people above includes:

- the non-dom's spouse or civil partner
- their partner if they're unmarried provided they are living together as though they were married or in a civil partnership
- their children aged under 18
- their grandchildren aged under 18

Unmarried couples aren't usually caught within these definitions, but they are for this purpose. 'Relevant people' also includes connected trusts and companies.

If you wanted to use this technique now you would need to transfer to family members that weren't caught by this definition and ensure that no 'relevant people' benefited from the transfer.

Note that the anti-avoidance rules in this area are very wide and can apply where overseas income or gains are transferred to anyone overseas. Therefore gifts from overseas family members to the non-dom or UK 'relevant people' can still be caught, even if the overseas family members are not on the above list. There can still be a remittance if the non-dom or 'relevant people' can benefit in the UK.

Is it still worth having capital and income accounts?

Yes it is if you are opting or may opt for the remittance basis in the future (and pay the £30,000 annual charge).

If you were taxed on the arising basis and could use the remittance basis in the future it would be advisable to keep UK taxed income or gains out of the overseas capital and income accounts to avoid mixing up taxed overseas income or gains with unremitted and untaxed overseas income or gains.

You would though need to keep separate pools in any case to track the income overseas that has been subject to the £30,000 tax charge.

Is it worth separating income and capital if I'm claiming the arising basis?

No, not unless there was any prospect of you claiming it in the future.
If you're opting for the arising basis all income or gains in that year would be taxed and the capital/income accounts would have no impact on this other than making reporting easier. Any income credited to the income account would be taxed as would any capital gains in the capital account.

Should I have separate income and capital accounts if I'm using the £2,000 exemption?

If the remittance basis applies then separation could be useful. This would apply whether the remittance basis is claimed or applies automatically (eg where the overseas unremitted income and gains are less than £2,000). This would be useful mainly in terms of different overseas sources, eg identifying pre-existing capital etc.

Can pre-existing capital still be brought into the UK free of tax?

Yes it should be and this should be kept in a separate account.

Can I avoid the £30,000 tax charge by losing UK residence?

Yes. You can use the remittance basis without paying the £30,000 annual tax charge until you have been UK resident for more than 7 of the previous 9 tax years. Once you exceed this you'll need to either stop using the remittance basis or pay the £30,000 in addition to tax on anything remitted (other than to pay the £30,000 tax charge).

Is non UK domicile status still beneficial for tax purposes?

Yes. It has numerous inheritance tax advantages as well as allowing the option of claiming the remittance basis. There is also the option of retaining income or gains of up to £2,000 per tax year overseas free of UK tax.

Can I use reinvested or deferred overseas income to avoid paying UK tax?

Yes you can. If you invest in overseas investments with a nil income yield (eg zero type securities) there would be no income to tax and the arising basis could be used, avoiding the £30,000 tax charge. Provided any income was below £2,000 the remittance basis could even be used to retain the income overseas without it being taxed.

The investments could then be sold free of CGT after departure from the UK.

Offshore bonds can also be used to allow tax to be avoided during a period of UK residency.

I've heard about overseas Exchange Traded Funds (ETFs) – how are these taxed?

The investment into the ETF should be regarded as a purchase of an overseas asset. The general rule is that shares and securities are situated where they are registered.

This will usually be in the country where they were incorporated. If they are registered on more than one register then they are located where the principal register is located.

Therefore an overseas ETF should be a non UK asset. If you're a non-dom and claim the remittance basis (and pay the £30,000 tax charge if necessary) any income and gains would be assessed on the remittance basis.

How will the new rules affect non-dom employees of UK companies?

Any employees who perform their duties of employment in the UK or have UK resident employers would be taxed as usual on their salary. Any non-doms who work abroad for non resident employers would be subject to the new remittance rules.

This means that on first arriving in the UK a non-dom employee could claim the remittance basis and avoid UK income tax on the overseas employment income. The only drawback in most cases would be the loss of the UK personal allowance and capital gains tax exemption.

If they remain here for more than 7 tax years they would then need to consider whether to continue claiming the remittance basis or not. Unless the overseas employment income (together with the non-dom's other overseas unremitted income) that was not brought to the UK exceeded around £100,000 (assuming no other income) it would not be worthwhile claiming the remittance basis and paying the £30,000 annual tax charge.

Instead they'd be better off simply being taxed on the arising basis and subject to normal rates of UK income tax on their earnings.

What changes were made in the 2009 Budget?

The 2009 Budget announced a number of relatively minor amendments to the remittance basis. These include:

Tax Returns

Under the previous rules, if you have any overseas employment income you have to file a tax return. The new rules state that where you have:

- Overseas employment income of less than £10,000, and
- Overseas bank interest of less than £100

you will not have to file a UK tax return, provided the overseas income is subject to a foreign tax.

Exempt Assets

The exempt assets rules allow anyone who is subject to the remittance basis (either by claiming it or by virtue of having unremitted overseas income/gains of less than £2,000) to bring some assets into the UK without them being classed as a remittance.

This includes personal items (eg watches, jewellery etc) and also certain items that cost less than £1,000.

Prior to the 2009 Budget you needed to have purchased these items out of overseas investment income for the remittance to be free of tax. The 2009 Budget changed this so that even if the assets were purchased out of overseas capital gains or overseas employment income they can still qualify for the remittance exemption.

The Budget is also backdating this new rule to April 2008.

Unremitted Income or Gains of Less than £2,000

The remittance basis applies automatically where you have unremitted overseas income or gains of less than £2,000.

The legislation will be amended to make this extra clear so that a claim will not be required in these circumstances. Essentially a non-dom will be treated as having used the remittance basis unless they notify HMRC that they wish to be taxed under the arising basis. Again this will be backdated and will apply from 6 April 2008.

UK Income of Less than £100

The provisions will also be extended to ensure that the remittance basis applies automatically where a non-dom has total UK income or gains of no more than £100 which has been taxed in the UK, provided they make no remittances to the UK in that tax year.

Gift Aid Donations

The 2009 Budget provisions confirm that if the £30,000 remittance tax charge is payable this is treated as a payment of income tax or capital gains for UK tax purposes. As such this would ensure that charities could claim tax relief even if the only tax you (as the donor) pay is the £30,000 remittance charge.

What changes were made in the 2010 Budget and 2010 Emergency Budget?

In the 2010 Budget there was a very minor addition to the definition of 'relevant person'.

The 2010 Budget stated that the tax legislation will be amended to clarify that a subsidiary of a non UK resident company, which would be a close company if it was resident in the UK, will be treated as a relevant person for the purposes of the remittance basis.

This applies as the original legislation did not specify that such a company would be a relevant person. Without this amendment it could have been argued that using overseas unremitted income for the benefit of a non-resident subsidiary did not amount to a remittance.

There were no specific provisions targeting non-doms in the June 2010 emergency Budget. However, as a result of the change in Government following the May 2010 election, there is less certainty for non-domiciled individuals.

The coalition agreement between the Conservatives and Liberal Democrats states that: "We will review the taxation of non-domiciled individuals" and this statement was reiterated in the June 2010 Emergency Budget.

Before the election the Conservatives toyed with the idea of introducing a £25,000 levy on anyone claiming non-domicile tax status.

Crucially this tax charge would apply irrespective of the length of time spent resident in the UK. Under the current non-dom rules you are only subject to the £30,000 tax charge if you have been UK resident for more than 7 years and claim the remittance basis.

The Liberal Democrats would like to clamp down on non-doms even further. Their election manifesto stated that:

"In addition we will reform the system of 'non-domiciled' status, allowing people to hold such status for up to seven years; after that time they will become subject to tax on all offshore income in the same way as domiciled British citizens."

At present we don't have any further information about what format any changes will take or when they will take place.

How much overseas income do I need to make it worthwhile paying the £30,000 charge?

As we've seen, non UK domiciliaries who have been UK resident for more than 7 of the last 10 tax years will be subject to the new £30,000 remittance tax charge, if they claim the remittance basis.

The key question for many is: 'When is it worthwhile for a non-dom to claim the remittance basis and pay the £30,000 charge?'

As there's a choice whether the £30,000 charge is paid or not (as you can always opt to be taxed on the arising basis and avoid it) it's useful to consider the break-even point at which it's worthwhile opting for the remittance basis (and paying the £30,000 charge).

Here are the general rules:

- If you have just overseas capital gains, the break-even point as a higher-rate taxpayer would be £107,143. This is calculated as:

  £107,143 x 28% = £30,000

  In addition, the annual exemption of £10,100 would be lost by claiming the remittance basis. When you add this to the calculation, the minimum overseas gain you would need before it is worth paying the £30,000 tax charge would be £117,243.

  Note that what we are talking about here is not an overseas capital gain of £117,243 but an overseas UNREMITTED capital gain of £117,243.

  Any gain that is remitted back to the UK would be taxed in addition to the £30,000 tax charge, so you would need to have an overseas gain that was kept abroad of at least £117,243.

  Note that the above assumes that you have other UK or overseas remitted income that uses up your basic-rate band.

  If you have no other taxable income, any gains would be taxed at 18% up to £37,400 (the basic-rate band for the current 2010/11 tax year). Above this they would be taxed at 28%.

  In this case you would need to have unremitted gains of at least £130,600 before it would be worthwhile claiming the remittance basis and paying the £30,000 tax charge:

	£
Overseas Gain	130,600
Less Annual Exemption	-10,100
Gain	120,500
Tax at 18%	6,732
Tax at 28%	23,268
Total tax	30,000

- If you have other taxable income (i.e., UK income or overseas remitted income) which uses up your basic-rate tax band you would be taxed on any overseas income at 40% if you opt for the arising basis.

  Therefore you need to have overseas unremitted income of £81,475 before paying the £30,000 tax charge makes sense.

In other words:	£
Overseas Income	81,475
Less Personal allowance	-6,475
Income	75,000
Tax at 40%	30,000

  If you had overseas unremitted income of more than £81,475 the £30,000 tax charge is less than the tax you would pay if you opted for the arising basis.

- If you had other taxable income in excess of £150,000, you would need to have overseas unremitted income of at least £60,000 to make paying the £30,000 charge worthwhile.

  You would lose the benefit of the personal allowance, whether or not you claim the remittance basis, and would be taxed at 50% (£60,000 x 50% = £30,000).

- If you have no other taxable income any income would be taxed at 20% up to the basic rate limit (£37,400). Above this it would be taxed at 40%. In this case you need to have unremitted income of around £100,117 before it would be worthwhile claiming the remittance basis and paying the £30,000 tax charge:

	£
Overseas Income	100,117
Less Personal allowance	-6,417 (restricted)
Income	93,700
Tax at 20%	7,480
Tax at 40%	22,520
Total tax	30,000

Pay Less Tax!

...with help from Taxcafe's unique tax guides and software

All products available online at **www.taxcafe.co.uk/books**

How to Avoid Property Tax
By Carl Bayley BSc ACA

How to Avoid Property Tax is widely regarded as *the* tax bible for property investors. This unique and bestselling guide is jam packed with ideas that will save you thousands in income tax and capital gains tax.

"A valuable guide to the tax issues facing buy-to-let investors" - THE INDEPENDENT

How Tax-Free Property Investments
By Nick Braun PhD

This guide shows you how to double your investment returns using a variety of powerful tax shelters. You'll discover how to buy property at a 40% discount, paid for by the taxman, never pay tax on your property profits again and invest tax free in overseas property.

Using a Property Company to Save Tax
By Carl Bayley BSc ACA

This guide shows how you can significantly boost your after-tax returns by setting up your own property company and explains ALL the tax consequences of property company ownership.

How to Avoid Tax on Foreign Property
By Carl Bayley BSc ACA

Find out everything you need to know about paying less tax on overseas property. Completely up to date with key UK and overseas tax changes.

Property Capital Gains Tax Calculator
By Carl Bayley BSc ACA

This powerful piece of software will calculate in seconds the capital gains tax payable when you sell a property and help you cut the tax bill. It provides tax planning tips based on your personal circumstances and a concise summary and detailed breakdown of all calculations.

Non-Resident & Offshore Tax Planning
By Lee Hadnum LLB ACA CTA

By becoming non-resident or moving your assets offshore it is possible to cut your tax bill to zero. This guide explains what you have to do and all the traps to avoid. Also contains detailed info on using offshore trusts and companies.

The World's Best Tax Havens
By Lee Hadnum LLB ACA CTA

This book provides a fascinating insight into the glamorous world of tax havens and how you can use them to cut your taxes to zero and safeguard your financial freedom.

Tax Saving Tactics for Non-Doms
By Lee Hadnum LLB ACA CTA

This unique tax saving guide explains in plain English the new tax rules for non-domiciled individuals that allow you to keep money offshore and tax free.

Using a Company to Save Tax
By Lee Hadnum LLB ACA CTA

By running your business through a limited company you stand to save tens of thousands of pounds in tax and national insurance every year. This tax guide tells you everything you need to know about the tax benefits of incorporation.

Salary versus Dividends
By Carl Bayley BSc ACA

This unique guide is essential reading for anyone running their business as a limited company. After reading it, you will know the most tax efficient way in which to extract funds from your company, and save thousands in tax!

Keeping It Simple
By James Smith BSc ACA

This plain-English guide tells you everything you need to know about small business bookkeeping, accounting, tax returns and VAT.

Selling Your Business
By Lee Hadnum LLB ACA CTA

This guide tells you everything you need to know about paying less tax and maximizing your profits when you sell your business. It is essential reading for anyone selling a company or sole trader business.

How to Avoid Inheritance Tax
By Carl Bayley BSc ACA

Making sure you adequately plan for inheritance tax could save you literally hundreds of thousands of pounds. *How to Avoid Inheritance Tax* is a unique guide which will tell you all you need to know about sheltering your family's money from the taxman. This guide is essential reading for parents, grandparents and adult children.

The Investor's Tax Bible
By Lee Hadnum LLB ACA CTA

This tax guide can only be described as THE definitive tax-saving resource for stock market investors and traders. Anyone who owns shares, unit trusts, ISAs, corporate bonds or other financial assets should read it as it contains a huge amount of unique tax planning information.